These Stones Cry Out

By

Adrienne Hartman

Copyright © 2015 Adrienne Hartman

All rights reserved

Contents

Chapter 1	Randy McPherson	1
Chapter 2	Kaia Kloster	3
Chapter 3	Cindy Tripp	7
Chapter 4	James Power	11
Chapter 5	Alan Greene	15
Chapter 6	Vicki Greene	19
Chapter 7	Hunter Beard	21
Chapter 8	Mike Nichols	23
Chapter 9	Paul Millman	27
Chapter 10	Pastor Melissa Fletcher	29
Chapter 11	Allen Ludens	35
Chapter 12	Jerry Dahmen	39
Chapter 13	Brian Balster	43
Chapter 14	Charlie Sanders	47
Chapter 15	Pastor Barbara Becker	51
Chapter 16	Barbara Elkjer	55
Chapter 17	Pastor Kirk Flaa	61
Chapter 18	Pastor Al Peratt	65
Chapter 19	Marty Jackley	71
Chapter 20	Pastor Mark Halford	73

Chapter 21	Grant Gomez	77
Chapter 22	Rick Scarborough	81
Chapter 23	B. Chad Connelly	85
Chapter 24	Leon Brech	89
Chapter 25	Chris Updegraff	91
Chapter 26	Kurt and Gina Schiferl	95
Chapter 27	Carla Noe	99
Chapter 28	Todd Schlekeway	103
Chapter 29	Tony Perkins	105
Chapter 30	Tracey Eberhard	109
Chapter 31	Shantel Krebs	115
Chapter 32	Denae Baustian	117
Chapter 33	Paul Baustian	123
Chapter 34	Jeff Kuper	125
Chapter 35	Jenna Haggar	129
Chapter 36	Cashimaria Stroud	131
Chapter 37	Russell Willingham	135
Chapter 38	Jim Bolin	141
Chapter 39	Vivian (Shillander) Ellis	145
Chapter 40	John Glasser	153
Chapter 41	Sue Mutziger	155

Chapter 42	Pastor Kenneth Hunt	161
Chapter 43	Glenna Remington	165
Chapter 44	Pastor William (Bill) Duncan	169
Chapter 45	Donna Seaton	175
Chapter 46	Matt Gasson	179
Chapter 47	Terrie Fischer	183
Chapter 48	Freida Fossum	187
Chapter 49	Rosemary Eliason	191
Chapter 50	Edith Gwien	197
Chapter 51	Gary Allen	201
Chapter 52	My Brush With Death	203

Introduction

When my first book of testimonies, "Living Stones", hit the top ten best seller list at a local Christian book store, I took it as a sign from God that He wanted me to continue to share His good news through my writing. So once again I set about finding people who were willing to share their stories with me. Sometimes I invited them to my house and interviewed them here. Other times I interviewed them over the telephone because they were far away in other states such as California, Texas, Florida, and South Carolina. I felt God inspiring me to give the second one this name – "These Stones Cry Out". I believed this title would catch a person's eye when they walked by the books in the book store. I also decided to make some improvements with this one. I included a table of contents and at least one Bible verse to accompany each testimony. I also wrote the testimonies of several nationally known leaders in order to pique the interest of more people across the nation, hoping this would give them the desire to pick up a copy of the book and read it. Lastly I included a prayer at the end of the book so people would have an opportunity to invite Jesus into their hearts and lives and be forgiven of their sins. My prayer for this book is for it to be an instrument to encourage and inspire others. My goal is to see lives changed for the glory of God. If you, who read this book, are a Christian please prayerfully consider getting a copy of it for a loved one, neighbor, fellow employee, or friend who needs Jesus in their lives. You probably have been praying for them for a long time and this book could be an answer to your prayer. In conclusion I want to personally thank everyone and especially those with very busy schedules such as Tony Perkins and Rick Scarborough for taking the time to allow me to interview them. Each one who shared their stories with me will receive a special blessing from the Lord because I believe their testimonies will touch lives all over the nation and, God willing, in other countries as well.

Chapter 1

Randy McPherson

Colossians 3:17 - And whatever you do in word or deed, do all in the name of the Lord Jesus, giving thanks to God the Father through Him.

Randy was raised in a Christian home with his father being a pastor. He, the oldest of seven children, was born in Minneapolis. When his father accepted a pastoring position in Neilsville, WI the family moved there. Randy accepted Jesus as his personal Lord and Savior at the young age of five and he has always felt God's loving hand upon him to keep him from straying away.

As a teenager, Randy felt God wanted him to follow in his father's footsteps to become a pastor but after he entered a Bible College to prepare, he sensed a shift in direction. God was leading him to go into the business field instead. So Randy started a business called Abra Auto Body. When he sold the business after 12 years, it had grown to 50 locations in 10 states and was grossing 65 million dollars a year. Since that time, Randy started and grew several more companies including real estate and signs. During this time, however, Randy had a desire to be involved in ministry. He began to see how God could use his businesses as a platform or springboard to do just that.

Randy was an avid believer in tithing and giving to missions both here and abroad. Because God could trust him with the money, He caused his businesses to prosper so he could give more and also travel around the nation and to other countries to speak. He considers himself more of an inspirational speaker than a motivational one. He constantly exhorts people to put Christ first in their businesses. Because he has a great love for the outdoors, Randy connects very well with sportsmen and women. At his events he will often give away bows that his brother makes and some of them are worth over a thousand dollars.

Randy wasn't always successful in business, however, in spite of the fact that he put his trust in God. He made mistakes and one of them cost him over 12 million dollars. His failure made the local and national news. However God was faithful and soon brought him back to prosperity.

Randy shared with me a high point in his life when he overheard a pregnant woman speaking to a friend about an abortion she was planning on having. Her doctor had advised this because x-rays showed a badly disabled baby. Randy went up to the lady and advised her to trust the Lord with her pregnancy. She took his advice and trusted God daily. Six months later she gave birth to a beautiful healthy baby girl. It was a lesson Randy never forgot. He tries to live out Colossians 3:17 every day. "When you live like this," he explains, "God will do powerful things."

Chapter 2

Kaia Kloster

Matthew 14:28-29 - And Peter answered Him and said, "Lord, if it is You, command me to come to You on the water." So He said, "Come." And when Peter had come down out of the boat, he walked on the water to go to Jesus.

This is how it was for Kaia. God asked her to get out of the boat and trust Him. Here is how her story begins. She was born and raised in a Christian home. Her father was a biologist and her mother was a nurse. As a scientist, Kaia's father struggled in his mind to reconcile science with faith in a God he could neither see nor touch. When Kaia entered college, she too was bombarded with many worldly ideas and unbiblical theories such as evolution. While she did remain a Christian, her walk with Christ was not a close one. She wound up with a PHD degree in cardiovascular physiology. As a research scientist and a busy mother, it was easy to put her faith on a back burner. However her Christian mother had a strong influence on Kaia as she grew up and it wasn't easy for her to shake it off. Her heart kept turning towards God. Her strong desire for the truth along with many questions concerning faith drew her back to church. A hunger for God kept gnawing at her heart.

Kaia was married by this time and had two children. She loved horses and eventually she and her husband bought a farm where she would have room for them. They also became involved in a small country church. It was here that Kaia began to walk more closely with the Lord.

During one particular summer, there were two instances when the Lord brought children to her farm and Kaia took them horseback riding. These children came from troubled backgrounds. Kaia's eyes were opened to her own abundant blessings as she discovered the powerful impact that time in the presence of horses could have on these youngsters. It provided a perfect opportunity to listen as these children began to open up and share their hearts with her. By now Kaia had grown enough in her faith that she could minister to them. She discovered how a seed had been planted for her to use horses to reach young people with the message of the gospel.

As Kaia absorbed more of the Bible, she started having inner struggles with her job. There always seemed to be some conflict deep within that she wasn't able to resolve. God was tugging at her heart to quit her career and to totally trust His leading. Finally Kaia gave in to the Holy Spirit's prompting and, like Peter, took a step of faith out of the boat and onto unknown waters - leaving her position in research to pursue a horse-based ministry.

Kaia's faith grew by leaps and bounds as she began a vigorous prayer life along with searching the scriptures for the deep nuggets of truth she longed for. In her journey, she met someone who was involved with Handi-Riders, which specialized in using horses to help those with disabilities. Kaia sensed God wanted her to help expand the programs for people with disabilities as well as to reach out to disadvantaged youth. Eventually HorsePower came into being through this merger.

Kaia shared how difficult it was at first. She no longer had the good income she had gotten as a researcher. There were months without pay followed by even more with sporadic income. Kaia learned to depend totally on God for all her and her family's needs, as well as the necessities of HorsePower. At times her circumstances looked very bleak. But God always came through. It was very difficult to carry on the work at HorsePower without a tractor and yet they couldn't afford one. However God saw the need and He moved on the hearts of some people to provide them with one. Another time they needed $30,000 to carry on the work of the horse camp. The Lord answered that prayer as well. As Kaia could see God's mercy and provision, her faith continued to grow and she would tell others about everything He did.

This has been a humbling experience for Kaia as she has come to realize that nothing good ever happens because of anything she has done but what God has done in and through her. The ministry at HorsePower continues to be a work of faith because no one is ever turned away because of the inability to pay. Kaia knows that every need will be met because she serves a God who always provides.

Kaia can't stress enough the vital importance of prayer and staying in the Word. She continually encourages people to step out of their boats and follow wherever God would lead them. She doesn't know where people's hearts are at but she hopes that her words of encouragement will make a difference in their lives and that perhaps somebody else will come along to take them further along in their journey with the Lord.

Chapter 3

Cindy Tripp

Romans 8:28 - And we know that all things work together for good to those who love God, to those who are the called according to His purpose.

Cindy was raised on a farm outside of the city of Sioux Falls and attended school in Harrisburg for 12 years. Although she was raised in church she felt that something was lacking in her life. Later on when she got involved in youth ministry it practically took over her life. Her focus was on the ministry instead of God.

God began to move in Cindy's life in ways that eventually caught her attention. In 2004, she was involved in a car accident. Shortly after that, she was diagnosed with fibromyalgia - a disease that affects the muscles and soft tissue. Cindy struggled with muscle pain and fatigue and stress as a result. Her health continued to decline and life became an almost impossible burden until she realized that she had been in control instead of turning everything over to God. Finally she relinquished her will and turned to Jesus Christ, allowing Him to take over the reins of her life. A peace she had never experienced warmed her inner being and she embarked on a new adventure with her Lord. She had always struggled with a hot temper but she discovered herself being delivered from this day by day.

Cindy and her husband took another step of faith and began attending another church a friend had told her about. To leave where she had attended all her life and step into new waters was frightening but she felt compelled by God to do so. She finally knew why as she experienced her faith growing enormously. Although she stills struggles with her health she has learned to trust God through it all and as a result has been able to manage it through medication and rest.

Cindy began her salon, The Upper Cut, years earlier but because of her illness has had to retire from it. She now only does hair for four ladies one day a week. She is still able to do the things she enjoys but has learned her limitations. Due to the fact that she has to spend a lot of time resting at home, she has been able to minister to people more. Cindy shared with me that when she began a ministry called The Gathering Place a few years earlier, she met a young woman who was in need. This lady had a small child and a boyfriend whom Cindy showed the love of Christ. Through meeting some practical needs in their lives, she has opened the door to share Jesus with them. She has invited them to attend the church where she goes and has been praying that they will eventually open up their hearts to Him.

Cindy told me about some of the obstacles that stood in the way of her being able to start The Gathering Place, a place where people and groups can go to get away for a weekend. At times it seemed like the door was closed but then God would open it again. One of the struggles was the lack of parking but then someone who owned several spots stepped up and offered five of them to Cindy.

Cindy shared how God has worked in her life through tragedy. Her mother passed away from cancer when she was only 60 years old. Cindy had prayed for two years, asking God to cure her. When He didn't answer that prayer, Cindy questioned Him. "Why didn't You heal her because she was such a good person?" she cried. At first the answer didn't come. But then she found herself visiting her father more. She had never been very close to him growing up. Cindy had always gone to her mother when she wanted to share anything personal. Now circumstances forced her to relate to her dad more. Her visits to the farm to see him increased and their relationship began to blossom until she really got to know him as a person. They grew to be very close until his death later on when he was over 80 years old. **Romans 8:28** became very relevant to Cindy.

As Cindy grew in her knowledge of God and how He has worked in her life, she doesn't forget to thank Him when she comes to Him each morning in prayer.

Chapter 4

James Power

2 Timothy 4:8 - Finally, there is laid up for me the crown of righteousness, which the Lord, the righteous Judge, will give to me on that Day, and not to me only but also to all who have loved His appearing.

Born in Huntsville, AL in 1967, James grew up in a Christian family where daily devotions were practiced each evening. Warm memories of these days fill his mind as he thinks about the times when he prayed with his parents at the early age of 5 or 6.

James has sad memories as well. His father, an engineer for NASA often traveled here and there by plane. One day he got the terrible news that his father had been killed in an accident while flying home. James was only 10 years old at the time and this incident hit him particularly hard as he was very close to his father. Christians from his church and community all reached out to James and his mother with loving arms of compassion and support and this helped them to get through this difficult period in their lives. Although his mother never married again, James was surrounded at church by Godly men who set good examples of how Christian men should behave. This was particularly helpful to him as he was growing up.

After graduating high school, James went to law school in Atlanta and served at a law firm there. During this time, he got involved with an incredibly dynamic church. It was here James felt a calling to enter the ministry so he moved to Dallas where he attended a seminary. This was a tremendous experience for him and it was here where he met Lara, also a student. After graduating, the couple married and went to Minneapolis where James got involved as an assistant pastor over the adult ministries. He also aided other ministries in the church as well as counseling people.

When James and his wife were expecting their second daughter,

Katherine, they decided to move to Sioux Falls in 2006 to be close to Lara's family. Despite not practicing law for 5 years, he began applying for legal jobs because it seemed like the best opportunity to find work in Sioux Falls that would allow Lara to stay home with their young girls. Then an amazing thing happened. One of the firms he interviewed with was the Woods Fuller Law Firm. Unbeknownst to James, an attorney at Woods Fuller was working on a South Dakota case with Dennis Withers, James' supervising partner from Atlanta, GA. James hadn't been in contact with Dennis for 10 years and so hadn't thought of listing this man as a reference because of the lengthy period of time that had passed by. But Dennis's firm in Georgia was listed on his resume so Woods Fuller asked Dennis about James, and Dennis highly recommended him for the job. It is the only South Dakota case Dennis ever had! James realized that God had led him to this city for a reason and this incident didn't just happen by coincidence.

James recalls many times when God has intervened in his life, either to protect or guide him. He is thankful because he remembers making bad decisions in his life from which the Lord rescued him. James recalls one such incident when he got on the wrong bus in Philadelphia and wound up in a very dangerous part of the city late at night. He stood, nearly paralyzed by fear for at least 20 minutes while waiting for another bus to come along and return him to a place where he could catch the correct one. He was very thankful for God's arm of protection that night.

He is blessed by his three daughters who display their faith in many ways. His youngest daughter is the most outspoken about her love for Jesus. James is happy that his girls are involved in a very good children's ministry at his church.

I asked James how he came to the decision to run for the circuit judge position here. He relayed his reasons to me in this way. Having been involved in Bible studies as well as serving as a pastor at a church, James understands that a person's life can have a great impact on another person. He believes a judge can cause someone to view police and the law in either a positive or negative way. If a judge isn't prepared for a case and is unethical or biased, he can leave someone with a sour taste in his mouth. It can have a profound effect on someone that may change his life forever. One the other hand, handling a case professionally and saying the right words to someone facing criminal charges can encourage them to turn their life around in a positive way. Therefore, James feels he is called of God to compete for this position of circuit judge in order to fulfill what he considers to be a ministry and not just a job.

Since my interview with James the election has come and gone. He lost the election but plans to continue running for vacant spots until he realizes his dream of becoming a judge.

Chapter 5

Alan Greene

Eph 2:8-9 - For by grace you have been saved through faith, and that not of yourselves; it is the gift of God, not of works, lest anyone should boast.

Born and raised in North Carolina, Alan grew up in a Christian home where he was taken to church and Sunday school and taught right from wrong. He considered himself to be a Christian because he knew about God and the Bible but he never realized it had to be a personal decision until later on in life. "There comes a time when a person has to evaluate Christianity for themselves and take it as a first-hand faith," Alan declares. This was something he never did until after he got married. He met the girl of his dreams when he moved to Sioux Falls while still in high school. A year after graduation, he married Vicki. This was all in God's plan as Alan was to learn what it really meant to be a Christian.

Vicki came home from a Christian women's meeting and said, "When we get to Heaven....." Alan didn't catch the rest of her statement as these five words jabbed at Alan's heart. He began to question whether or not he would get there after he died. Soon after this, he went to a Christian Businessmen's meeting where he listened to a man share his testimony. Toward the end of his talk, the speaker challenged everyone with a question. "If you died today, do you know you'd go to Heaven? Do you have assurance of eternal life?" These words haunted Alan for several days until he went for a walk in a field outside of town to have a talk with God. He had always believed in the right things and could recite a creed but he had come to the realization that he never had a personal relationship with Him through Jesus Christ. Humbled and broken, Alan admitted he was a sinner, confessed it and told God he wanted to turn from his sin and surrender his life totally to Him. From this day on, life became a journey for Alan as God took him to places he never fathomed of being.

Alan and Vicki had a great love for music and one night, they went to a concert where they were further challenged with their faith. The event wasn't advertised as being a Christian one but halfway through, the singer surprised everyone by declaring his faith in Christ. He shared that he had a Christian gospel album so Alan and his wife hurried to the Christian bookstore to buy a copy. They began studying Christian music and lyrics using the Bible. Alan understood more and more what the Bible meant by a spirit-controlled life, not just on Sunday but every day.

Alan shared with me how God used situations to break his pride so he would understand that Jesus was in control. He shared a struggle that he and his wife experienced, a mountain that I will elaborate on when I share Vicki's testimony.

In the 1980's Alan and his wife along with two other couples started up a music ministry in which Christian concerts were promoted at the arena and other places. After their children came along, God impressed on them to give this up so they could focus more on their family. Later on, there was to be another big "marker," as Alan called it, which would lead to another leap of faith.

In 1998, Alan took his wife and children to Juarez, Mexico. They were all humbled and impressed by the Christians they met there. Though these people lived in poverty, they expressed a vibrant faith through which the light of Jesus shone. When they returned home, God began to impress on Alan's heart, "Take the church outside the walls. Bring light into the darkness. Bring the body of Christ together." He and Vicki prayed and asked God what He meant by these words and what it was that He wanted them to do. God spoke His Word into Alan's heart from **John 8:12** - "I am the light of the world. Whoever follows me will not walk in darkness but will have the light of life." They began to envision a large gathering of people where music was used to reach them for Christ. So in 1998, the first Life Light Festival was launched and it has continued to this day. Every Labor Day weekend big Christian bands and speakers are brought in to a large field outside of a little town in South Dakota where hundreds of thousands of people of all ages and denominations go to hear the good news of Jesus Christ. The ministry has grown from humble beginnings into a national and global one today.

Alan says that the longer he walks with God, the more he recognizes that it is a journey of faith. For every Christian who has surrendered his or her life to Jesus, God has a purpose for. **Ephesians 3: 20** - Now to Him who is able to do exceedingly abundantly above all that we ask or think, according to the power that works in us.

Chapter 6

Vicki Greene

Romans 8:38-39 - For I am persuaded that neither death nor life, nor angels nor principalities nor powers, nor things present nor things to come, nor height nor depth, nor any other created thing, shall be able to separate us from the love of God which is in Christ Jesus our Lord.

Vicki was born and raised in Sioux Falls where she was nourished in a loving family who taught her about Christ. But it wasn't until, years later, when she began attending a Christian Women's group that she realized she needed to make a personal decision to follow Jesus. Vicki had come to terms that Jesus death on the cross was a free gift, one she would never be able to earn through doing good. Performing good works was to come after receiving Jesus into her heart and then she would perform them out of gratitude of what the Lord had done for her. She went home to share her new knowledge with her husband, Alan.

Vicki loved children and was planning on starting a family after she and Alan were married for almost three years. Yet God had different plans and it wasn't to be. After seeing a doctor, they were confronted with the devastating news that they probably would never be able to have children of their own.

Vicki, along with Alan, got on her knees and sobbed out a prayer of brokenness to God. "Lord, we have surrendered to You. You tell us in Your Word that You will give us the desires of our heart," they cried. "You know we have a desire to have children but if it's not Your will for us, please take away the desire."

It was only a few short days after that prayer that they received a phone call from the adoption agency to come and pick up their brand new baby girl. A couple years later, God gave them two natural born girls. Vicki shared that this was the greatest joy in her life - to be able to raise these three children to know the Lord. Today they are all grown and Vicki is blessed with four grandchildren with whom she can share God's love. While raising the girls, Vicki never had any desire to home school them. However God had different plans. The oldest one who was in kindergarten at the time pleaded with Vicki to home school her. Vicki finally relented and promised her that she would as soon as she was ready for middle school. She told herself it would be only for a year and that would be it. God must have chuckled when He saw what was really in Vicki's heart. She not only home schooled the oldest daughter but she wound up doing this for all three.

Vicki shared with me how the Mexico mission's trip had such a huge impact on them all. Today the girls are all involved in the Life Light Festival ministry using the gifts God has given them. One is an artist, another a musician and a third one is a prayer warrior.

"When I trust God instead of doing things my own way, they always work out," Vicki says, "but when I forget to do that I make mistakes." Vicki feels humbled to have this big ministry but she emphasizes, "God doesn't call the equipped. He equips the called." It is all about Him and not us, she stresses.

This is what Vicki and Alan Greene believe and share with others.

I John 5:11-13 - And this is the testimony: that God has given us eternal life, and this life is in His Son. He who has the Son has life; he who does not have the Son of God does not have life. These things I have written to you who believe in the name of the Son of God, that you may know that you have eternal life, and that you may continue to believe in the name of the Son of God.

Chapter 7

Hunter Beard

Psalm 46:10 - Be still, and know that I am God; I will be exalted among the nations, I will be exalted in the earth!

Hunter was born and raised in Pittsfield, IL. As the son of a pastor, he came to know Jesus at an early age. He described this experience as a feeling of heavy chains which were binding him falling away and setting him free. He enjoys the support of his family and church which keep him on the right path. Hunter loves the relationship with his family during devotions at night. During this time, his dad will help him understand difficult passages in the Bible. Hunter particularly loves the story about Peter walking on water because it teaches about faith.

I asked Hunter what challenged his faith the most. He told me that listening to bad language at school all the time tempted him to fall into the trap of swearing. However the strong Christian influence at home and church along with the power of the Holy Spirit has kept him from going down that road. He also mentioned a young lady, Kristen, who works with him at church to video tape his father's sermons on Sundays. He described her as being like a sister to him, one he never has been blessed with in his family.

Like a typical teenager, Hunter likes to absorb mac and cheese, chocolate milk, coke and tacos. He also enjoys playing catch with a mitt and baseball with his dad. His biggest love in the outdoors is hunting. In the fall he will go with his dad and sometimes his grandfather on a big deer hunting trip. "It teaches patience," Hunter explains. "You have to wait quietly for hours in one spot for a big buck to come along." But he doesn't mind because he gets to drink in the peace and stillness of God's creation and meditate on His goodness.

Hunter, as a teenager, displays the attributes of being a strong leader. He has inherited the positive attitude and gift of encouragement from his dad. From the time he was small he has accompanied him along with his mother to visit patients in hospitals and nursing homes to encourage them as well as pray for them. He specifically remembers a time back in Illinois when he went with his parents to visit a terminally ill cancer patient. They all prayed for her and she was miraculously healed. Hunter also tries to reach out to fellow students at school by inviting them to attend youth group with him at church. Two of them have accepted his invitation and are presently attending.

God has shown His love to Hunter by giving him dreams. God spoke to him one night and warned him to stay surrounded by strong Christian friends and remain faithful to his church. In this way, he wouldn't yield to temptation and fall away into the sins of the flesh and the world.

Chapter 8

Mike Nichols

2 Corinthians 5:17 - Therefore, if anyone is in Christ, he is a new creation; old things have passed away; behold, all things have become new.

Mike was born in Canton, SD, one of eight brothers and sisters. He grew up in a poor family with an abusive and alcoholic father outside of Canton in the small town of Beloit, IA. Although he never heard the good news of Jesus Christ's birth and resurrection in his home, he was privileged to attend a Sunday school and a school where the Bible was taught. School was held in the same building as church services were. It was here that Mike's teacher introduced him to Christ. Before class sessions began each morning there was prayer and Bible reading and the Pledge of Allegiance was recited. Mike told me his family didn't own a car so his mother would walk him along with his brothers and sisters to Sunday school each week.

Mike was used to hard work on the farm since he was ten years old. In high school, he took a job at a meat market. He also worked as a welder in the summer. Despite the fact that he worked hard, he got involved in drinking and smoking and running with a tough crowd. After graduation, he attended college where he began using drugs heavily as well as drinking. In his last year of college he met Peggy whom he would marry. Although Peggy was a very devout church goer and never smoked or partook of alcohol or drugs, she didn't have a personal relationship with the Lord. This, coupled with the fact that Mike kept drinking heavily, caused the first six years of their marriage to have a lot of strife in their home. But God was about to bring a drastic change into their lives.

In 1977, Mike and Peggy attended a Lowell Lundstrom crusade. When the altar call was given, they went forward to give their lives to Christ. Mike remembers holding their infant son in his arms as he prayed the sinners' prayer. Both Mike and Peggy were radically saved and their lives and marriage were never the same since. Mike told me it was particularly miraculous that Peggy's heart was reached as she was bound by religion and church tradition that didn't allow for a personal relationship with Jesus.

Due to emotional pain caused by abuse he endured as a child, Mike continued to drink for two more years. He admitted, however, the drinking wasn't so much because of the emotional pain but more because of selfishness. Then he and Peggy got involved with a group of vibrant spirit-filled Christians who discipled them and got them into the Word of God. Mike began to devour the scriptures like a ravenous wolf. When he read verses about a need to forgive others, Mike realized God was commanding him to release the unforgiveness that he held against his father. He also came to realize that since God forgave him for his sins, he also needed to forgive himself. When he obeyed, he was totally set free and alcohol no longer was a crutch in his life. The Bible became so real to Mike that he knew he had to start sharing it with others. So for the past several years he has taught the Bible to others and especially to young people. Mike has a burden for them because of all the worldly pressures these teens and college age people endure. He doesn't want them to fall into the same traps of the devil that he had been imprisoned by.

Mike has a successful business today but he keeps Jesus first. His heart's desire is to be pleasing to God and effective for Christ with the time he has left on Earth. His main goal is to hear Jesus say, "Well done good and faithful servant!" when they meet face to face. As a disciple of Christ, he is committed to loving his wife as Christ loves the church. He and Peggy have committed to raising their three sons in the ways of the Lord. Now they have stretched their Godly influence towards their five grandchildren.

In his business he strives to deal honestly with others even though they don't always return his integrity and faithfulness. He chooses to forgive those who have been dishonest towards him. Because he does this he has experienced the peace of God that goes beyond all understanding. He challenges other Christians to do likewise and to live contrary to the world system. In that way they can have that relationship with God that Mike desires for everyone. In fact this is what he has devoted his life to - to see others set free and begin to live a joyful, peaceful life in Christ.

For over 35 years, Mike has expressed his praise to God by playing a guitar in Christian bands.

Matthew 6:33 - But seek first the kingdom of God and His righteousness, and all these things shall be added to you.

Chapter 9

Paul Millman

Philippians 4:13 - I can do all things through Christ who strengthens me.

Paul was born and raised on a farm outside Flandreau, SD along with three brothers and two sisters. It was a happy Christian home where he enjoyed life working and playing in the pure clean air. Although Paul learned about God and the Bible, it wasn't until he was in high school when, at a movie theater, he decided to commit his life to Christ. This sealed his relationship with the Lord.

Paul first met and dated his bride to be, Lori, in high school. After he graduated he followed his desire to join the Navy yet Lori waited for him for nearly four years until they married. They moved to San Diego for a while but missed the farmlands of South Dakota and so returned after a few short years.

Tragedy shook Paul's faith when his mother died of cancer at only 54 years of age followed by the death of his oldest brother from a massive heart attack only two years later. Paul began questioning God. Why would He allow this to happen to two of the nicest people one could ever meet? It just didn't make any sense. He felt a distance from God after that until he and Lori started a family. Three beautiful daughters spaced two years apart caused Paul's trust in God to be renewed. He watched his girls all become strong in their faith. "That is what I call success," Paul declares.

Devastation once again visited Paul when his eldest daughter, Abigail, lost what would have been their first grandchild and only six months later, her husband was killed on an oil rig in North Dakota. Paul was amazed at his daughter's resilience through it all and he attributes this to her strong trust in God and an unyielding belief in family strength and love. She knows that the separation from her baby and husband is only temporary and they will be reunited one day in Heaven. Paul shared with me that he and his family lifts one another up often, understanding God's support for them.

In 1991, Paul and Lori along with another individual began Interim Healthcare, a home healthcare service that allows the sick and disabled to remain in their own homes. They service 300 people from the newborn to the very elderly. "Home is where one feels most secure," Paul says. All three of his daughters have worked in the business, performing various tasks.

Sometime after Paul retired from the Navy, he had a life-changing experience. He woke up in the night feeling like an elephant was sitting on his chest. Being a nurse, Lori knew something was very wrong and rushed him to the hospital. It was a good thing she did. It turned out that Paul had a blood clot in his lung. These clots typically form in the legs and move up into the lungs and heart and people who experience this most often die. In fact only 15% survive this condition. This was indeed a miracle. Apparently God had further plans for Paul.

Paul calls Lori his rock and he is very happy in his occupation as Administrator of Interim Healthcare. Philippians 4:13 is his favorite Bible verse and he thinks of it each time he faces a challenge.

Chapter 10

Pastor Melissa Fletcher

Jeremiah 29:11 - "For I know the plans I have for you," declares the Lord, "plans to prosper you and not to harm you, plans to give you hope and a future."

This is the story of Melissa's life, a tapestry woven by God's own hand. She was born in 1971 to an unwed mother of 17 years of age who lived in Dell Rapids. Desperate, this 17-year-old girl didn't know where to turn. Her well-meaning friends urged her to get an abortion, thinking a baby would ruin her chances for a decent future. Finally she turned to the pastor in the church in which she had been raised. He advised her to give the baby up for adoption in order to save face in the church and the community. Hurt and devastated she left the church and put herself into foster care in order to save her mother from shame. When her mother (Melissa's grandmother) found out how she was being abused in this place, she begged her to come back home. The grandmother, being of strong faith and a powerful godly influence in Melissa's life, knew that He had a plan and purpose for the baby so she and her mother decided to raise her.

When Melissa was six years old, her mother married and it was one of the most joyful days of Melissa's life. They lived on a farm where her adoptive father raised sheep. It was here that God began to call Melissa into His service. At this tender age, she would go into the barn with the sheep and hold "church." She stood at a pretend pulpit and preached to the animals. Melissa would often reflect on Bible passages that talked about Jesus being the great Shepherd and we His sheep. Unbeknownst to Melissa, God was preparing her to become a pastor years from then. Her parents seldom went to church but made sure that Melissa and her siblings got there so they would drop her off at the door each Sunday. In 5th grade, she got to go to Bible camp. It was an experience she would never forget because it was here that Jesus became very real to her.

However when she got to high school, she struggled between living out her faith and going along with her friends in worldly ventures. She wanted to be baptized but struggled with the idea because she felt there was too much sin in her life. Finally at the age of 17 she decided to take this step.

Because Melissa felt abandoned by her biological father, she found it very difficult to get very close to anyone. Any relationship she had was very guarded for fear that they would leave her as well. This went on for many years and even her walk with Christ was hindered because of it. One day her biological father passed away from a massive heart attack at age 45. At the funeral she met him for the first time as she gazed at him in his casket. Melissa was moved by the physical similarities between him and herself. When she was being introduced to members of his family (people who never knew Melissa even existed) she began a healing process. The woman her deceased father was supposed to marry became a good friend to Melissa. She hoped she could establish a relationship with her paternal grandparents as well but because of situations in the past, it wasn't to be.

In 2000, Melissa married Chad Fletcher who turned out to be a blessing and a godsend to her. Although he was raised in a different denomination, God used him to continue the healing process in Melissa's emotions and soul. Soon after their marriage Melissa found herself expecting their first child. When she was only a few weeks into her pregnancy, she experienced serious symptoms of miscarriage. Frightened she called her doctor who was a Christian and he prayed for the Fletchers. That night they went to bed thinking that they had lost their child. However, the next day, Melissa got an ultrasound and it showed a heartbeat. She was overjoyed as she realized God had answered their prayers and Hannah was born in 2001. In 2003, a second girl was born and they named her Kathryn.

Because Melissa wanted to be of the same faith as Chad, she went through many classes for a year. This caused her to dig deeper into her own soul and to understand what she believed and why. After living in Sioux Falls for a while, the couple moved back to Dell Rapids where they got involved with Chad's church. Melissa had a strong desire to teach but was turned down because of the fact that she hadn't been born into that faith. Despite her disappointment, the Lord began a new work in Melissa. When she was at home on maternity leave with her second daughter, a lady who was working as her replacement called her and gave her a message from God that Melissa was being called into the ministry. Melissa doubted at first because she felt unworthy of such a calling. But she decided to pray about it and as she did she experienced a personal revival. A powerful thirst for the Lord empowered her as she felt a holy fire taking place within. She was so transformed that her husband noticed a change. As a result, he had no problem when Melissa felt God leading her back to the church of her childhood.

At her home church, the pastors quelled any doubts Melissa had concerning the calling God had on her life. "You are like a diamond in the rough," they told her. "God will take you and mold you into a thing of beauty. He doesn't call the qualified. He qualifies the called." As they encouraged her to follow God's leading, Melissa prayed and sought after Him with all her heart. She stepped out in faith by taking a baby step. She decided to explore the seminary by taking a few basic classes. When her mother-in-law was diagnosed with a malignant brain tumor at this time and given only a couple years to live, she, along with the entire family, was devastated because she had been like a matriarch. She questioned why God would allow this to happen now of all times. But God whispered to her, "My time isn't your time and My ways are higher than your ways." Melissa hung onto that and when her mother-in-law passed away only six months later, she had received Jesus into her heart along with many of the relatives on Chad's side of the family. She understood then what God was doing and why.

When Melissa was attending seminary classes, she got her first opportunity to preach in the church when the pastors were away one Sunday. She had no idea what she would preach about but after much prayer, she felt led to preach about Peter stepping out of the boat to walk on the water. How often Melissa was able to relate to that in her life! She prayed to God asking Him to affirm His call on her life. That week, Melissa's daughter, Hannah, who was now three years old, drew a picture for Melissa. Hannah said, "Mommy, Jesus wanted me to draw you this picture." When Melissa asked her, "What did you draw for me?" Hannah replied, "It's a picture of Jesus hugging you because you finally got out of your boat." Hannah had drawn two stick figures hugging, water and a boat. The amazing thing was, Melissa had not told anyone what she was planning to preach on that week but God spoke through a child to affirm His call on her mother's life. After that, in 2007, the pastors left the church, leaving Melissa in place as an interim pastor. The people loved her so much they elected her to be the lead pastor in June of 2008.

Melissa shared with me several miracles that happened over the years since she married. At the age of two, Kathryn exhibited all the symptoms of leukemia so they took her to the hospital to be tested. Melissa was fearful of losing this child so she put her on a prayer chain. She and her husband spent much time on their knees in prayer asking for healing for this child. After that Kathryn had no more symptoms and was given a clean bill of health. She and Joshua, a son born later on to the Fletchers, had a lot of problems with gastric reflux. Kathryn was on medication and Joshua, as a baby, would vomit the milk up that he ingested. Desperate, Melissa took the children to a healing service and both were miraculously healed. Melissa also experienced healing for severe migraines which baffled the medical team that had been following her case. She told me about so many things God has done in her life that there simply isn't room to share them all here. However I want to tell you that her children are all very close to God. They have all given their lives to Christ, and some have talked to angels and even to Jesus Himself. They have a very strong faith and discernment and one of the girls has been called to be a pastor. One last thing Melissa shared with me I have to tell you because it speaks of love and forgiveness.

Melissa's parents returned to church and, in 2007, she had the opportunity to baptize her mother. What a joyful day that was! Another miracle was when the pastor who had hurt her mother so many years before came for a visit to the church and asked forgiveness for all the harm he had done. Restoration was brought about and hearts were mended. This is an awesome way to end this testimony. So never underestimate what God will do...with Him all things are possible.

Chapter 11

Allen Ludens

Luke 6:38 - Give, and it will be given to you: good measure, pressed down, shaken together, and running over will be put into your bosom. For with the same measure that you use, it will be measured back to you."

This is a promise that Allen has always lived by since giving his life to Christ. And here is his story.

Allen was born in Sioux Falls and grew up on a farm nearby. He was the oldest of eight children and the family was poor. They had to make do with patched up and mended clothes but the children were always clean and well fed. Allen attended a small country school. When he was in the 1st grade, there were only five other students in attendance. He graduated from Lennox High School in 1965 among 35 seniors. After that a family friend offered to pay for Allen's college education but he turned it down. Instead he chose to enlist in the Marine Corps shortly after his 18th birthday.

The picture of an ad stating the Marines wanted a "Few Good Men" stuck in his mind as Allen headed off to boot camp. His heart beat in anticipation as he left to be with the "badest and the best." He had no idea at the time that he would be thrust in the infantry with a "front line" company in Viet Nam. When a live grenade landed beside Allen's head but didn't explode, he started to realize that God's hand of protection was upon him in spite of the fact that he was living away from Him and drinking heavily. Allen was able to recall another time when God spared him. He tried a reckless maneuver with his car which should have killed him but never even got a scratch.

After his hitch in Viet Nam, Allen was stationed in Oklahoma where he met Sharon who would later become his wife. She had been raised in a small Bible believing church where her father had been serving as a deacon. At the time Allen met her, she was in a backslidden condition. However after they married, Sharon felt she should return to church and this decision caused Allen to start questioning the things of God. Off and on he attended the little church with Sharon and he also talked to the pastor with a series of questions about the Bible. Allen had observed how the pastors always held alter calls after each service. One evening at a service, Allen answered one of those calls and this started him on the right footing that would later lead him to becoming a very successful business man.

Shortly after that the Ludens moved back to South Dakota where Allen fell back in with old friends and began drinking again. During this time, his father unexpectedly died at the age of 43 from a heart attack leaving his mother and five children alone on the farm. Since Allen's father was his best friend this hit Allen particularly hard causing him to spiral further downward. Besides drinking, he turned into a workaholic. Having been raised on a farm, he was no stranger to hard work so he dove into it like a maniac, sometimes going for days without sleep. Then on Sundays he would sleep for twelve hours or more.

Later on God moved some of Sharon's friends into Allen's life to draw him back into church. It was there when Allen answered the call to rededicate his life to Christ. At this time, he continued to drink until he had a Damascus Road experience. It was as though the Lord had put His hand on Allen's shoulder and spoke softly to him. "Son, you can continue to drink all you want but if you do it will cost you everything including your life." That was a point of turning and Allen hasn't had a drink for close to 40 years.

The Ludens were blessed with three sons and two of them work with Allen in his business. Years earlier he had been diagnosed with an abnormal degeneration in his spine and placed on disability. This allowed Allen the time to do what he always enjoyed doing and that was going to auctions to buy things and then reselling them. It eventually led him to open his own business. The lion's share of it is selling new trailers from various manufacturers.

In 2001 Sharon passed away from cancer. In his loneliness, Allen married again but it wasn't God's will for him and it ended in divorce. The experience of losing his wife and later on having to deal with a divorce left him wandering in a spiritual desert. Then he met the woman God had chosen for him. Today he is blessed to be happily married again to a beautiful wife.

God has given Allen the gift of giving and he has discovered that the more he gives, the more he receives. His business has won rewards and recently Allen has learned that he is next in line for the President's Award because he has consistently been in the top ten for sales in the nation. Allen knows that he can't take the credit for his success because it is all God's doings. God is faithful to bless those who give because He can trust those who are good stewards with His money. "We can't out give God," Allen states.

Chapter 12

Jerry Dahmen

Hebrews 6:17-18 - Thus God, determining to show more abundantly to the heirs of promise the immutability of His counsel, confirmed it by an oath, that by two immutable things, in which it is impossible for God to lie, we might have strong consolation, who have fled for refuge to lay hold of the hope set before us.

Hope is what Jerry has learned and it is what he seeks to establish in others through his daily radio broadcast called "I Love Life." He didn't always love life, however, and there was a point in his own life when he had lost all hope.

Jerry's story begins when he entered life in 1949. As a child he stuttered badly and even though he had dreams of one day being a radio broadcaster it seemed hopelessly impossible because of his speech impediment. Jerry was persistent, however, so at the age of twelve he sought out the help of a speech therapist. After two and a half years he was able to overcome his handicap. At the early age of fifteen, he realized his dream when he acquired his first job in radio at KISD, a station which is no longer on the air in Sioux Falls.

Later Jerry moved to Nashville where he got involved as a radio news director for the Grand Ole Opry's WSM Radio. He was married with three sons during this period of his life. Over a span of many years, he enjoyed the honor of receiving over 100 major awards for broadcasters. In spite of this, his life took on a sudden downward spiral. His career in Nashville came to a screeching halt and his marriage hit rock bottom as well. The stress of it all landed him in the hospital with a heart condition.

Jerry sank into deep despair which triggered thoughts of suicide. One day he entered a store where he bought a Magnum handgun and then went back to his apartment to end it all. It was Christmas Eve and he held the gun to his head, squirming for the courage to pull the trigger when he heard the voice of a pastor on the radio that had been playing at the back of the room. Pastor Dave, a friend who was a recovering crack cocaine addict was sharing his testimony. A verse from the book of Psalms reached Jerry's heart through the airwaves. "Give Thanks to the Lord for He is good. His love endures forever. The Lord is with me. I am not afraid. The Lord is with me. He is my Helper." This propelled Jerry to lay down the gun and make his way to this pastor's church the very next Sunday. While there, he sought Pastor Dave out and told him what had been going on in his life. He shared with him how he had this radio program called "I Love Life" during which he had interviewed thousands of people about how they had overcome adversity in their lives. Pastor Dave urged Jerry to listen to these stories he had recorded over the years to remind himself about how these people had triumphed over the many overwhelming problems they had faced. Jerry heeded his advice. He realized light and darkness could not abide in the same place. He chose to live in the light and put all the despair and negative thinking behind. So Jerry filled his mind with the Word of God, knowing his mind was like a computer. He reminded himself of the old adage (Garbage in! Garbage out!) and he was determined to reprogram his thinking.

Today Jerry has forgiven his ex-wife and is continuing his career back in Sioux Falls as news director of KXRB Radio. He has chosen to walk in faith. "Faith is more than words but it comes from the inside out," he says. Jerry has shared it through his radio broadcast and has heard back from many how the stories they have heard has encouraged them. Jerry also wrote a couple of books that tell the stories of how people have come through adversity victoriously.

Jerry leaves us with Six Spiritual Principles of Successful Living.

1. If you dwell on the darkness, you'll never see the light.

2. Take the focus off of you.

3. Fill your mind with Godly thoughts.

4. Forgive and let go.

5. Lighten up.

6. If you can't change your circumstances, change your attitude and make it an attitude of gratitude.

Chapter 13

Brian Balster

James 4:13-17 - Come now, you who say, "Today or tomorrow we will go to such and such a city, spend a year there, buy and sell, and make a profit"; whereas you do not know what will happen tomorrow. For what is your life? It is even a vapor that appears for a little time and then vanishes away. Instead you ought to say, "If the Lord wills, we shall live and do this or that." But now you boast in your arrogance. All such boasting is evil. Therefore, to him who knows to do good and does not do it, to him it is sin.

Brian was born into a family with a long Christian heritage on both sides. He was raised on a farm outside Gann Valley, SD where he learned that his great grandfather was a circuit riding preacher who traveled on horseback from town to town to share the gospel to all who would listen. Brian recalled the day when he was eight years old and particularly naughty. After being chastised by his mother, he fell at her knee and responded to the Gospel as she led him in a prayer to receive Jesus into his heart.

Brian during his sophomore year in high school decided to take his life with Christ more seriously and make a solid commitment to follow the Lord. This was when he felt a calling to go into some form of ministry. He then went to Sunshine Bible Academy and then on to Bible college. After graduating from West Bible College in Littleton, CO, he worked with several ministries. By now he had a wife and four daughters.

In 1998, Brian began his first business in Platte, SD. Topps Manufacturing Co. was very successful and as the business thrived, Brian developed a bloated ego, forgetting who was really in charge. God had to teach him a lesson and so the business began to fail. Profits dwindled and the debt was overbearing until Brian was faced with failure. Overwhelmed and broken, he turned to God for answers as he relinquished his business to

Him, knowing he couldn't keep things going on his own. After praying, he felt led to sell the business in order to pay off the debts. He retained only the Retriever Product part of the business but was left with nothing else so had to start over. This time, Brian was determined to do things God's way. "Lord," he prayed. "I am willing to go through every door You open but close the ones You don't want me to enter." This began an adventure that Brian never fathomed.

A door opened and Brian found himself traveling to Haiti to encourage the Christians there. He was amazed that such impoverished people had so much joy but he knew the source of their happiness came from their faith in Christ. He returned home to step through another door only four days later. This time he went along with an older gentleman as a travel companion to Kenya. This was to be the beginning of a new ministry to the people over there. As a lay pastor, Brian visited several churches to preach. Several pastors took him aside to ask him to help them go to Bible College. Although Brian wanted to help them in this way, he knew it just wasn't feasible. There just wasn't the money to do so and it would be detrimental to the churches for their pastors to be away so long. Brian went home to pray with a friend about this. There had to be some way to help these people grow in their knowledge of the Word. As they prayed, God gave them an idea. Why not go back to Kenya to hold teaching conferences for the pastors and church leaders there! So they did! It was a success so they did this three more times and are now planning another trip in July of 2014.

During the times Brian was in Kenya, he was burdened by the fact that so many people were getting sick from polluted water. He wanted to do something about it so he recently went to Texas to learn how to drill wells by hand. What he learned he plans to carry back to Kenya to teach the people there.

Brian wanted to make improvements to his retriever product but was frustrated with the fact that he wasn't able to come up with a better design that would work. This product is a tool that is attached to road graders. When Brian went back to Kenya, he shared this concern with a pastor who offered to pray for him. Brian returned home to pray about it some more. One night he got a vivid dream that displayed a perfect design for his product. He woke up and knew this idea was from God. When Brian tried it out, it worked perfectly. His sales have improved as a result.

God has supplied all of Brian's needs in order to carry on the work in Kenya. His church, along with three other churches, has come alongside to help with the finances in order to provide Bibles and other necessities to carry on the ministry there. Brian is very thankful for the salvation Jesus has provided on the cross and his heart's desire is to see others come to a saving knowledge of the Lord both here and abroad. He knows that by meeting the practical needs of the people in Kenya, it provides a platform for him to share the gospel with them in meaningful ways.

Chapter 14

Charlie Sanders

Acts 9:15-16 - But the Lord said to him, "Go, for he is a chosen vessel of Mine to bear My name before Gentiles, kings, and the children of Israel. For I will show him how many things he must suffer for My name's sake.

Charlie was born in Georgia, an only child who was raised in the church. Shortly after giving his life to Jesus at the age of 13, he got mixed up with the wrong crowd and began drinking. By the time he got into high school, his drinking had escalated and by his senior year he was experimenting with marijuana. In spite of all this, however, Charlie was involved in sports and managed to get a football scholarship to a college in Georgia.

Miraculously, Charlie excelled in football in spite of his heavy drinking and partying. His girlfriend got pregnant so Charlie and she decided it was for the best that she got an abortion. This left an indelible scar on Charlie that hasn't completely been erased to this day. Then in his sophomore year, Charlie's grandmother died unexpectedly. Angrily Charlie accused God of being unfair because she had been the backbone of the family. In his bitterness, he turned his back on God and continued in his sinful lifestyle.

During his junior year, Charlie began dating Carrie Williams who would years later become his wife. They had a son together but this didn't stop Charlie from his partying, drinking or doing drugs. Instead he progressed from marijuana to cocaine. In spite of his wild life, God's hand of protection remained upon him. Charlie recalled instances when he overdosed and should have died.

Charlie continued playing football and he got the opportunity to do a professional football workout in Georgia. This caused him to give up drinking for a while but then he teamed up with the wrong people and fell back into it.

In 2010, Charlie had the opportunity to go to Billings, MT to play indoor football. Of course he jumped at the chance so he packed up and moved there, leaving Carrie in Georgia. At this time he stopped the drinking and the drugs and began reading the Bible, seeking God's help. It wasn't long, however, when Charlie began hanging around bad company again and this led to a split-up between Carrie and himself. By this time, he added pain pills to his list of drugs and alcohol.

One day, Charlie began having physical problems such as swollen lymph glands and pain in his kidneys. Thinking he had Chlamydia he went to a medical clinic where he tested negative. Relieved he got up and got dressed and was ready to leave when the doctor stopped him. He gave Charlie the bad news that he may be suffering from H.I.V. The doctor prescribed some medicine but told him it probably wouldn't help. In shock, Charlie went home and called Carrie to let her know what happened. She broke down in tears. When he confessed to his roommate how he had messed up his life and relationship with Carrie, he told Charlie that God could turn his life around. Then he told him the story of Saul (later called Paul) in the Bible and how he had sinned so badly against God by persecuting the church. Yet God had a plan for Saul and called him to become one of the greatest Apostles that ever lived. (**Acts 9:1-22**) After hearing this, Charlie was so touched in his soul that he picked up his Bible and ran outside where he cried his heart out to the Lord for three hours. "Lord, please give me one more chance and I will totally give my life to You," Charlie pled. His physical symptoms immediately vanished and Charlie got up off his knees an entirely new man.

Charlie returned to Georgia where he married Carrie and they immediately got involved in the church. They prayed for God to place them where He wanted them. After that, they moved to Sioux Falls with only $500 in their pockets. After visiting a few churches they found one where they felt God's love and they knew that this was to be their church home. It was here where an evangelist prophesied over Charlie, saying that God would use him in ministry - a platform to lead people to Christ.

In October 2013, Charlie was asked to work full time in student ministry. Then in January 2014, he began working with Collision of First Priority. This ministry does reach-outs to the students in all the public high schools in Sioux Falls. Student leaders help to build relationships with their peers and then they are invited to Bible studies and other events. First Priority is there to come alongside these leaders to help them out wherever needed. Many students have come to Christ and at one event there were 67 kids who made decisions for Jesus. Charlie told me that First Priority is always looking for people to help them and anyone who has a heart for teenagers is welcome to volunteer.

In June of 2014, Charlie will celebrate his 4th anniversary of being free from drugs and alcohol. He is planning to start training to become a pastor through Global College online. His story proves that no matter how far people fall into sin, God can still pick them up and radically transform them for His use in His Kingdom.

Chapter 15

Pastor Barbara Becker

Romans 10:13 - For whoever calls on the name of the Lord shall be saved.

Barbara was born in 1953 to a family who was bound up in alcohol. Her father worked as a miner in Wallace, ID, a little mining community, and her mother, a musician, played in a bar. In 1959 the family moved to the Uranium boomtown in WY where Barbara stayed until she graduated High School in 1972. Barbara's parents didn't go to church but they made sure their children went on Christmas and Easter. Hopelessness, fear and rejection were all she knew as she followed after her parents' example by becoming involved with alcohol and then drugs. This resulted in an out-of-wedlock pregnancy that led to a bad marriage. Drunkenness, violence and abuse brought terror and misery to Barbara for four years until she finally escaped with her life to wind up in Grand Forks, ND.

For a while Barbara lived off the streets with nowhere to go. She hated herself. She hated men and she even hated women for allowing men to abuse them. She moved from there to Watford City, ND for what she calls a chance to change, but only continued in the same cycle of addiction. Fear and rejection haunted her day and night until she was on the verge of suicide. By now she had three children and was reaching out everywhere for help. She hung on to the dream for change but it never came. A visit to a counselor, however, left her feeling more suicidal than ever. Deep down inside, she was searching for God and somehow knew He was the answer. She would take her children to church in hopes that they would come to know God and not end up like her. Because of her past, she felt unwanted and that it was too late for her but not the children. Barbara blamed her drinking problem on her boyfriend and everything and everyone else because she wasn't willing to look herself in the face. After a night of drinking she visited friends that encouraged her to attend her first AA meeting. When she attended her first meeting she was faced with the stark truth that the root of the problem dwelt in her and until she quit making excuses for her drinking, she would never be free.

A visit to a counselor on October 3, 1985, however, left her feeling depressed and hopeless and more suicidal than ever. Deep down inside, she was searching for God and somehow knew He was the answer.

That same day a close friend who had a personal relationship with Jesus kept witnessing to Barbara but she wanted nothing to do with it. Things were about to change, however, when this friend took her to a second-hand store to shop. Barbara was in no mood for shopping but a book caught her eye. It was titled "Power For Living" and boy, o boy; Barbara knew she needed an answer for her life. She bought the book for a quarter and then went out to the car to read it. During the time her friend was still in the store shopping, Barbara devoured it cover to cover. This was when she made a wonderful discovery of the scripture **Romans 10:13** - "For whoever calls on the name of the Lord shall be saved". For the first time, she learned that salvation was a free gift and didn't have to be earned as she had been taught in the church of her childhood.

Barbara bought her first Bible called "The Book" and began reading it. Her soul thirsted so greatly after the truth that she locked herself away in the house for two solid weeks until she had read it entirely from Genesis to Revelation. As she was reading the book of Leviticus and crying out "Can anyone love someone like me?" the Lord revealed Himself and the power of His love, mercy and forgiveness. When she called her friend to tell her about it and that she had given her life to Christ, her friend was amazed. How could anyone read the Bible in just two weeks? This friend invited Barbara along with another friend and her pastor to come over to her house to pray for Barbara to receive the Holy Spirit. This had been explained to her by her friend as "just receiving more of Jesus". While the pastor was praying, Barbara had a vision where she saw the printed letters of Ezekiel and they were ablaze. This frightened her and she didn't know what to make of it. But her friend told her what it meant and that the fire of God was upon Barbara which was the Holy Spirit.

Barbara continued to read the Bible through four more times in the next three months. She simply could not get enough of the Word. God showed her that He put this thirst in her so that she would fill up the empty spots in her life and to be prepared for what He had for her in the future. Barbara also got involved with Women's Aglow where she received a lot of her spiritual training.

Barbara also started attending a church with loving pastors who encouraged her every step of the way. At this time she was still living with her boyfriend outside of marriage until one day the Holy Spirit convicted them that they needed to get married. When these pastors left, Barbara then began attending a new church that was just established in her city. It had been founded by pastors that had the oversight of other churches in the state. It was here that Barbara was trained further in how to minister to others. When the pastors at this church resigned in 2000, the founding pastors came to ask Barbara to take over as the next pastor. Barbara fervently resisted and made all kinds of excuses why she wasn't ready to do anything like that.

Then Barbara went to a five day Bible conference where God used a speaker to break down all her resistance. Every excuse she had made was shot down and she returned home ready to accept the calling God had for her. She no longer allowed fear and rejection to hold her back. The speaker's final words, "With God all things are possible. Just say yes!" reverberated through Barbara's mind over and over again.

On August 18, 2001, Barbara was installed as pastor. She still wrestles against the spirits of fear and rejection but she has learned to ward them off with the power of the Word, both living and written, which she continues to read today. "There is safety in numbers," Barbara shares.

"Stay close to your leadership and you will be fine." Her church in Watford City, ND is a nondenominational church which comes under the authority of the International Association of Ministries. They are Christ centered, Bible believing, and full gospel and their mission statement is patterned after Jesus' words, "For the Son of man is come to seek and to save that which was lost." It is a church with the desire to walk out the fullness of the word of God in our own lives and in doing so, affecting and making a living difference in the lives of those around us.

Chapter 16

Barbara Elkjer

Psalm 107:20 - He sent His word and healed them, And delivered them from their destructions.

In his gospel Luke tells of the day Jesus stood up in a synagogue and read from the scroll of Isaiah, "The Spirit of the LORD is upon Me, Because He has anointed Me to preach the gospel to the poor; He has sent Me to heal the brokenhearted, to proclaim liberty to the captives And recovery of sight to the blind. To set at liberty those who are oppressed; to proclaim the acceptable year of the LORD." (**Luke 4:18-19**) This is really Jesus' mission statement for His ministry. That was a very good day for Barbara Elkjer and everyone who has suffered abuse because Jesus heals the brokenhearted, sets the captives free, opens blind eyes and rescues the oppressed. Barbara's story is evidence that He does heal and restore through the power of the Spirit.

Barbara was born in Bemidji, MN which is located in the North Woods. This is still where her family loves to vacation in the summer time. Barb had a difficult childhood. Her mother was mentally ill with a condition called narcissism. This type of mental illness causes a person to be excessively self-centered and self-absorbed.   For a narcissist, it is all about "me" all the time.

While her father was finishing medical school at the University of Minnesota in Minneapolis, Barbara often wandered the very busy University Avenue with no supervision. It was not surprising that at the age of three, she was run over by a car. All the bones between her pelvis and her ankles were broken and she spent a year in a full body cast. This resulted in her left leg being 1-1/4 inches shorter than the right one. To compensate she was fitted with special built-up orthopedic shoes which earned her the taunt of "gimp" on the school playground. Barbara's hot temper caused her to lash out and fight. She was used to fighting with her older brother who was somewhat of a bully because of his neglect and abuse. As a matter of survival, Barbara became a very strong willed, independent and angry girl.

The family was quite well to do and belonged to the country club. Almost daily during summer vacation Barbara's father would drop her off at the country club around 9:00 AM and leave her there to fend for herself until he finished office hours for the day. She had to scrounge for food by eating the others' leftovers. Eventually she learned she could order food and charge it to her father's tab.

Barbara reflected that she didn't know which was worse - her mother's emotional abuse or the physical abuse. She related that her mother would beat her with anything in hand. However, the last time her mother beat her she hit Barbara with a glass bottle which broke on impact and cut a gash on her right cheek. She still wears the scar from it today. Sadly she recalled that, in her rage at seeing the blood, she punched her mother in her solar plexus and ran away from home for four days but her mother never hit her again.

Besides this, Barbara was sexually abused by another relative and her father never protected her from this atrocity. Her father was an ophthalmologist who escaped his mentally ill wife and the chaos of their home by absorbing himself in his medical practice. He would begin with surgery at 5:00 AM in the morning and finish with hospital rounds by 10:00 PM at night. Between her absent father and her neglectful mother, Barbara and her siblings were completely left on their own. She felt protective of her younger sister and would take her wherever she went as she didn't trust her being alone with her mother.

Throughout Barbara's life, God tried to reach her with His awesome love. She went to a church and parochial school where she first learned the scriptures. Often after school she would sit in the middle pew of the school chapel and drink in the peace and presence of God. This was where she had her first experience with the presence of the Lord. Because of the stress of abuse and neglect at 9 years old, she developed bleeding stomach ulcers. One day while sitting in the chapel, an overwhelming peace enveloped her and God healed her. Jesus spoke to her and assured her everything was going to be all right. Barbara shared that since then she has had an "iron stomach" and is now able to eat anything. During the birth of her first child she experienced the Shekinah glory of God filling the room like a golden, sparkling cloud. These experiences with God were what got her through those difficult years.

Later on as an adult, Barbara went to counseling. Her counselor told her that neglect is the worst kind of child abuse. It sends the message that the child is unwanted and unworthy of love and care. This brought some understanding to her but she was still unable to connect the dots with God. He continued to reach out to her but Barbara's fierce independence made it practically impossible for her to release her will to Him.

Barbara was married and pregnant with her second daughter when she visited a dear friend, Marcia Lawrence, who had been born-again. Christianity had left Barbara disappointed so she studied other religions extensively, but nothing seemed to fill the emptiness in her soul. During their visit Marcia challenged her to read the Bible one more time and then ask the Holy Spirit to reveal the truth to her. Barbara heeded her friend's advice and began to read the New Testament. Her eyes fell on the words in **Luke 9:20-21** where Jesus asked his disciples saying, "Who do you say I am?" Peter answered saying, "The Christ of God." This scripture flew off the page at her. It was as if God was asking her that very question, "Barbara, who do you say I am?" This was the point at which she surrendered to God. It was as if He took her up to the top of a mountain to show her His truth. She was humbled before Him and totally yielded her stubborn will to Him. Ever since, she has been chasing after Him and trying to keep up.

After reading about the Spirit, Barbara sought more from God and began seeking the baptism in the Holy Spirit. She took a trip out to California in her search. Upon arriving in San Diego she opened up a telephone directory and randomly chose the name of a church. It turned out to be Jerry Bernard's church. When Barbara called the church it just happened that they were hosting a three-day crusade where well-known healing evangelists Charles and Frances Hunter were ministering. Barbara was raised in a liturgical church where everything was quiet and orderly and no one expressed themselves during the service except to recite written prayers. But in this church people shouted in praise, raised their hands, and sang in tongues and this made Barbara very uncomfortable. However, she was drawn back to this Pentecostal church the second night. Francis informed the congregation that the Lord had told her earlier in prayer that He was going to heal backs that night. Too intimidated to join the healing line, Barbara waited until after the service to ask Francis to pray for her short left leg which was the source of her frequent back pain. Charles came and prayed for her and she felt God's power sweep over her. When she went back to the doctor after returning home, he confirmed to her that her legs were now the same length. By healing the physical damage that was caused by her mother's neglect and demonstrating the reality of the power of the Holy Spirit, God assured Barbara of His overwhelming love for her.

Barbara continued to pursue the Holy Spirit. She was searching for a good Bible study and got involved in one that was cultish. She received the baptism in the Holy Spirit but she knew error was being taught so she started searching for another Bible study. She found a good one, Bible Study Fellowship, which taught the truth about the Trinity. Yet, Barbara had been left with feelings of doubt concerning the reality of her experience with the Holy Spirit. She was determined to find the truth so went away for five days to fast and pray. She spent the entire time praying in her prayer language (tongues) and when she came back home, she had been forever changed. Barbara knew she had the truth and her experience with the Holy Spirit was true. God began moving in her life and her family and her walk with Jesus became so very real. She compared the experience of the baptism in the Holy Spirit to a wedding ceremony. The wedding only begins a life-long, intimate relationship that grows and deepens. It isn't just a badge you wear on your shirt to say, "I got it!" It is the deepening of your relationship with Jesus and the significant expansion of your relationship with the Holy Spirit.

God began to heal Barbara from all the hurts of the past. She learned how to forgive. She said that she had to learn to honor her mother even though she wasn't honorable. She discovered that the word "honor" in Hebrew means "weighty" or "heavy." The Spirit revealed to her that honoring means to consider the words or behavior of another person very seriously - very heavily - when choosing your own behavior. This means that she had to consider carefully what her mother had done and determine to be different - to allow God's truth to shape her thoughts and behavior instead of past pain. One day Barbara visited the old house where she had struck her mother after her mother hit her with the glass bottle. Standing in the very same spot, she repented and asked God to forgive her for striking her mother. Immediately she was set free to be totally healed from her painful past. Now Barbara has chosen to believe what God says about her, that she is loved and accepted. She no longer listens to the lying voices of the past.

God has called Barbara to become an ordained pastor and to pursue a PhD in theology. She will tell her students that God teaches us by the Spirit through His Word which is His textbook. But we can't pass the course until we work out the lesson in His laboratory of life. Barbara shared that every lesson in her life has always come with a lab where the truths of the Bible had to be worked out in real life with real people. This is true for every Christian who is walking with Him. God keeps His promises and Barbara is proof that He can restore damaged and broken lives.

Chapter 17

Pastor Kirk Flaa

II Corinthians 5:17 - Therefore, if anyone is in Christ, he is a new creation; old things have passed away; behold, all things have become new.

Kirk was born in 1962 to godly parents - Bryan and Bonnie Flaa. They had a strong love for one another and for their two sons - Kirk and Craig. Kirk describes his childhood as being very blessed. He remembers the family memorizing Bible verses, having daily devotions, and going to church regularly. Thus Kirk was saturated with the things of God.

Because his father worked for the government, they moved often. With each promotion they had to relocate. When Bryan had an opportunity to take a high position in Washington D.C., however, he turned it down. He didn't feel this would be a fit place to raise a family so they wound up in Galchutt, ND, where Bryan took over the family farm. Here Kirk attended his first year of high school. He loved it there on the farm with the fresh country air and all the opportunities for hunting and fishing. But it was here that Kirk gradually lost interested in God and was lured towards worldly activities. It began with his dropping out of Sunday school. His grandparents, Leonard and Geneva, who were a strong Christian influence in his life attempted to guide him back to the Lord. Geneva, who had retired from teaching Sunday school, offered to start again if Kirk would return. Kirk did but it lasted only a little while. To those who observed Kirk, he had all the appearances of being a very good kid but inside he was full of sin. His wild streak led him to alcohol and partying.

After graduation, Kirk attended Concordia College in Moorhead, MN and obtained a degree in secondary education. During his stint in college, he completely turned his back on God and his drinking grew worse. Though he was trained to be a teacher he never chose that occupation. Instead he got a job at Payless Shoes in Fargo where he met Gloria, his future bride. He was a manager trainee at that time and in May 1987, the couple married. For a year they lived in Denver but after that moved to Sioux Falls, SD where Kirk became a route driver for T. O. Haas Tire Co (now American Tire Distributors). He and Gloria became parents to two boys, Eli and Elliot. Kirk worked his way up to territory manager despite his habitual drinking. Everywhere he went he had a beer in his hand and was constantly drinking. Gloria became increasingly concerned about his drinking and the example he was providing to their oldest son, Eli, and warned Kirk she had bags packed and was prepared to take Eli and leave if his drinking did not change. Then there was a turn of events.

Late October in 1993, Kirk and Gloria were out for the evening. As usual, Kirk was partying hard and Gloria was very reserved. They were driving Kirk's company pickup. He had been drinking heavily and a police man pulled him over. It was discovered through a breathalyzer that he was twice over the limit to drive. Kirk thought the jig was up and that he would be hit with a D.W.I. This would mean the end of his job. The policeman, however, gave him a warning and would drop the charges as long as Gloria drove the rest of the way home. This had a great impact on Kirk.

The next morning as Kirk was driving to work, he pulled over to the side of the road with tears running down his face. "God, rescue me from myself," he cried out to the Lord. Immediately he was set free. All desire for alcohol left him and he began praising God. He praised Him for sparing him from being arrested with a D.W.I. He praised Him for just who He was. God worked a total about face in Kirk and he left his sinful life style to walk after God. He began studying the Bible prolifically. He also bought a Bible dictionary so he could study the meaning of words in the Bible. He memorized scripture and he grew amazingly with his walk with God. **2 Corinthians 5:17** became very real to Kirk.

Shortly after that, Gloria turned her life over to Christ and the couple became unified in Him. This resulted in a most blessed relationship.

Over the next several years, Kirk felt a tugging in his spirit to become a pastor. The calling grew stronger and stronger until he shared it with Gloria. Immediately she said, "No way!" She wasn't about to give up all they had, a beautiful home in the country and all the comforts of life they had enjoyed so Kirk could go running down some rabbit trail to who knows where. So Kirk just prayed and Gloria agreed to pray as well for God's direction. Kirk wanted God to speak to her about it if this really was His calling. A year went by and then one day outside the church, Kirk found Gloria crying her heart out. He wondered what was wrong and when he asked her, she answered, "We need to go to seminary."

So the couple sold their lovely home and Kirk quit his job and they set off to attend a seminary in Plymouth, MN. After three years of school, he interned at a church in Norway, IL. Not long after that, Kirk and Gloria were called to return to the church from whence they came in Sioux Falls, SD. Here they still minister and many people have been blessed through their ministry.

Chapter 18

Pastor Al Peratt

Psalm 40:1-3 - I waited patiently for the Lord; And He inclined to me, And heard my cry. He also brought me up out of a horrible pit, Out of the miry clay, And set my feet upon a rock, And established my steps. He has put a new song in my mouth - Praise to our God; Many will see it and fear, And will trust in the Lord.

This is a scripture that Pastor Al lives by to this day. And here is his story.

Al was born in San Diego, CA on April 1, 1948 at Coronado Naval Station. His family was very military and very strict. He describes the city as very beautiful but under the circumstances in which he was raised it was sunny on the outside but very dark in the interior. This is the case for anyone who is raised in an alcoholic family. Al and an older brother who remembers how it was back then attests to the fact that they were thrown around into six different foster homes over a period of eight years. Their parents both had drinking problems and later divorced. When his father remarried, Al was back in the home but his relationship with his step mother was poor. Because of a lot of bitterness and hurt, she would fall into fits of rage when she would beat Al with a belt after forcing him to pick out the hurtful weapon. He was most often guilty of lying or some form of shenanigan but there was one time he remembered when he was falsely accused. Due to the abuse, he began wetting the bed when in the 6th grade. His step mother used various forms of punishment from throwing him into the shower and forcing him to stay there while icy water gushed down onto his body to tying a placard on him with "Bed wetter" printed on the front and back. He had to wear it to school but a compassionate sister came to his rescue and gave him a sweater to wear over it thereby covering up the embarrassing disclosure.

One day, Al's father and step mother went forward in church to give their lives to Christ. Al saw a change in them in that they didn't drink or do drugs any more but there didn't seem to be any more love displayed in the home. All he saw was hypocrisy in the church. After going to a dance instead of the Youth for Christ meeting that took place each Saturday, Al's father set him up with a counselor at church. During his first session, he had a frightening experience. The counselor proceeded to lock the door to the room and then started fondling Al inappropriately. The sexual abuse and stalking continued for a year until Al threatened the perpetrator with bodily harm unless he stopped.

Despite the fact that Al, as a teenager, found solace in his school and church and was very active in the youth choir and youth group, he led a double life. He would lie and steal on the sly while, at the same time, lead the youth choir and Youth for Christ group. Nevertheless he attempted to serve God in his feeble way. After graduating high school he worked as a cook at a Christian camp during the summer in Santa Fe while waiting to attend seminary in the fall.

The first year of seminary went well but by the second year he started getting into trouble. He got involved with the wrong crowd and began drinking and doing drugs as well. When he got busted, everyone on the campus learned about it. Al was called up on the carpet but he lied when he promised to never do anything like that again. He fell back into drinking and was kicked out of the seminary. Bitterness overtook Al and he was determined to join the army and go to Viet Nam where he could take out his anger by killing the enemy. He was faced with disappointment, however, when he was assigned to type up records as a legal clerk. Even though he continued to drink and do drugs it wasn't until just before he was discharged from the army that he got busted. This was in 1971.

After his discharge, he went to Los Angeles to look up his biological mother. When he found her, he discovered he had more brothers and sisters. He moved in with them but brought 40 pounds of hashish along with him to sell. In the same apartment building he met an outlaw biker who helped him sell drugs. Another man called "T" also got involved in the racket. Because of all that was going on, Al's mother decided to escape it by moving back to Illinois where she was originally from. In the mean time, Al fell deeper and deeper into drugs until he began to sell barbiturates along with booze and pills. When a girlfriend who he had a baby with decided to dump Al for somebody else, Al turned his back on God. He became one of the members of the brotherhood which is the enforcement squad of the biker group. They would punish people who owed them money, were informants or just plain enemies. One night, Al was asked to go with them and leave all his weapons at home. When they arrived by car to Long Beach, each member was handed a gun. Al knew he was being asked to "punish" someone by murdering them so he said a foxhole prayer. Afterward he handed the gun back to the President of the gang and told him he wanted no part of that. They pulled the car over and told Al to get out. He obeyed and just stood there waiting to be shot. Instead of killing him, the President yelled at him and told him to get all his stuff together and leave town and never come back or he would be shot. Al gathered up all his belongings at the club house and hid out in LA until an army friend picked him up and took him back to San Diego.

In San Diego, Al sunk to new lows. He created a smuggling ring while running with an outlaw motorcycle gang. They had a racket of setting up gang members to get busted so they could pay off past debts. Al was caught up in one of these traps and wound up doing five years to life in Chino Prison. As part of his sentence, he fought fires at the fire camp. While in prison, Al realized God had spared him from committing murder. He also knew God was trying to get his attention. Would Al continue down the same road or would he turn around and serve God? But Al wasn't ready to make that commitment yet. He had been turned off by all the hypocrisy he saw in the leadership of the Christian community.

Instead of turning away from the drugs that had put him in prison, he continued where he left off after getting out. He now became addicted to heroin. After driving from his sister's house one night his truck went out of control and he wound up in a body cast for 18 months.

Nothing turned him back from the road he was on. Al continued the drinking, drugging, and riding for 14 more years. After that he was introduced to meth. His wife loved it but he hated it. But Al loved the money he made from it so this went on for another 14 years. One night he and his wife had a huge fight in which she took a butcher knife to him. Al described her as being very beautiful but tough. After the fight, he kidnapped his son and fled to an old girlfriend's house which was located in Rapid City, SD. She assured him there were no drugs or alcohol around but that turned out to be a lie. Nearby was a major motorcycle gang where Al would sneak off to for a beer and a joint. He wound up as their bar tender at a topless club in town. He eventually became manager there using all his time and talents God had given him for the wrong reasons. Eventually he got back with his wife. Al told her to go to the gang members there and get some meth to bring back to South Dakota. This created quite a dilemma with the two gangs so he used all the years of his gang savvy to keep the peace.

By the late 1980's, Al had taken over the meth trade in Sturgis, SD. This put a big bulls-eye on his back for other drug dealers, police agencies and the violent criminals around. To save Al from certain destruction, God stepped in and allowed him to get busted again. This time he was sentenced to seven years for distributing and three years for possession. During these years in prison he developed Hepatitis 3 and the early stages of diabetes 2. His body was badly beat up from the life style he had been leading. For the first nine months in prison, he didn't get a lot of sleep. He rented a light from the penitentiary by which he was able to read the only thing he could get his hands on - a Bible. **Psalm 40:1-3** became his rallying cry. To this day he lives by it and he teaches it wherever he goes. But before that happened, there was more that took place.

Al was charged with RICO, an organization that goes after the mafia and gang members in particular. He was faced with 160 years of federal drug crimes. Because the government was doing some illegal things, it was eventually reduced to 5 - 40 years of charges. Because of all the prison time Al was facing at 38 years of age, he figured he would die there. He knelt down in his prison cell and prayed, "Lord, I want to spend the rest of my life helping other people like me. I want to see them set free." God heard Al's prayer and he stood before a kind judge who reduced his sentence and allowed him to spend the rest of his time under house arrest. That meant he would be allowed to work and attend church. This took place in 1998. The gangs he had been involved in wanted him back but every year when he was urged to go back, Al would say, "Nope! I'm serving God now!"

Al has since been licensed twice and ordained twice, once by a church and another time by the Volunteers of America. Al has served as chaplain at the prison as well as Volunteers of America. While in prison, he got a business degree and a paralegal degree. He stresses the importance of a good education when he talks to the prisoners. He has also worked part time at Keystone Treatment Center and speaks there once a month. He has been married to his wife, Theresa, for 40 years. She was raised in a satanic home and never went to church. However she lived a couple of blocks away from a church that fed people each Friday night and helped clothe them as well. Through their kindness both she and Al were able to see the true love of Christ and have made the commitment to follow Him wherever He leads.

Al shared three specific miracles that have taken place in his life.

1. He was asked by Governor Janklow to be chaplain of the prison after sharing his story with him.

2. Al received a full pardon from President Obama.

3. Through spiritual storms and they will come, how will you react? Al gave an example of this. He was diagnosed with cancer and was treated with radiation and chemotherapy which killed all the white cells in his body. This resulted in his going into a coma for 45 days. The miracle was this. People from all groups and walks of life came to pray for him. One group in particular was full of the Holy Spirit and when they prayed, Al could feel the cancer being driven out of his body. Since leaving the hospital Al has improved. God still has work for him to do.

Chapter 19

Marty Jackley

Exodus 31:18 - And when He (God) had made an end of speaking with him on Mount Sinai, He gave Moses two tablets of the Testimony, tablets of stone, written with the finger of God.

Marty was born in Sturgis, SD where his father was both a professor at Black Hills College and the local state's attorney. Marty's mother was a teacher at Sturgis High School. He has a younger sister who is vice-principal at Stevens High School.

The family has always taken an active part in their church so Marty grew up in a stable, God-fearing home. His grandfather owned a farm 20 miles from Sturgis that remains the family farm.

Marty expressed his appreciation of the small town where he lives as it affords many opportunities for his son and daughter to be involved. His daughter plays the violin and his son the guitar. They are both very active in sports as was their father at an early age. Marty enjoyed track and other sports during his high school and college years. He holds a degree from the SD School of Mines where he graduated with honors in electrical engineering and received a Juris Doctorate from the University of SD where he studied law.

Marty's first job after law school was that of a federal law clerk. After that he entered private practice and became a partner in a Rapid City law firm. It was here where he met and married Angela, the love of his life.

Marty's career advanced and he eventually became US Attorney in SD which is the top federal prosecutor. Later on he became Attorney General in SD which is the top state prosecutor. Marty has faced many challenges in this position. He has recently been involved with the Hobby Lobby case and is happy to see the US Supreme Court defend their freedom of religion rights. Freedom of religion is very important to

Marty and because he carries a strong pro-life position personally he is happily engaged in protecting South Dakota's pro-life laws. His defense of these laws is on-going and he has enjoyed many successes thus far in protecting the constitutionality of the pro-life statutes. Presently he has been defending our State Constitution and statutory law which define marriage to be between a man and a woman. It has been challenged recently by two same sex partners married in Minnesota.

The Attorneys General community has been very involved in protecting people of their personal religious rights under the First Amendment of the U.S. Constitution. They along with Marty have been engaged in challenging Obama care which has brought too much federal intrusion into the states and individual lives.

Marty explained that the office of Attorney General doesn't allow him to get directly involved with personal lawsuits. However, he is often indirectly involved by protecting our State Constitution and other laws, thereby coming alongside to help in cases. I asked Marty what recourse do businesses have when they are being sued because hiring lawyers can be extremely expensive and therefore prohibitive for many small businesses. He told me that interested organizations such as the Liberty Counsel and the Chamber of Commerce often provide lawyers to protect them without charge in such an event.

Family and faith have been a guiding force in Marty Jackley's life. Both have been very supportive in the daily challenges he faces as Attorney General.

Today Marty is faced with more challenges because of the Supreme Court's decision which legalized same-sex marriage in all 50 states. This has allowed same sex couples to marry in South Dakota.

Chapter 20

Pastor Mark Halford

Romans 10:15 – And how shall they preach unless they are sent? As it is written: "How beautiful are the feet of those who preach the gospel of peace, Who bring glad tidings of good things!"

When one thinks of a motorcycle club, the first thought that comes to mind is a gang of hooligans who love to terrorize a neighborhood. This is not the case, however, with Mark Halford. He is the President of the Barbarian Motorcycle Club which is a club of Christian men who go all over to share the gospel with anyone who will hear. Here is his story.

Mark was born in Buffalo, NY and was the oldest of three children. He grew up in the suburbs with parents who were married to each other all their lives until death claimed them. So Mark enjoyed a stable environment in which he knew about God but didn't enjoy the personal relationship of knowing Jesus. This left him empty and searching. At the young age of 14, out of frustration, he ran away to Toronto, Canada where his stay was quite brief. The authorities soon caught up with him and returned him to his home. Drug use, criminal activity, and sexual immorality became part of Mark's life. Mark's parents had Mark put on probation, threatening to admit him to a reformatory if he didn't shape up; this was a wake-up call but not enough to fully change his lifestyle. Mark was an athletic boy and became concerned about his health so he decided to quit smoking everything. A decision was made by Mark that he would start living a healthier lifestyle but still something was missing. After Mark graduated from high school at the age of 18, he decided to give Houston, TX a try as he heard there was plenty of employment there. His visit in Houston didn't last long, however, and he knew absolutely nobody so he decided to return to Buffalo, NY.

After Mark returned to Buffalo he had a desire to get back to nature, thinking he could discover the essence of life. He avoided tobacco and alcohol and began to eat natural foods. He took up hiking and backpacking and soon landed a job in a state park. As Mark was leaving to take up residency at Allegany State Park in Southwestern New York State at the age of 19, he bought a Bible which he would check out occasionally. When he did, the Word jumped out at him and spoke to him as though God was speaking to him then and there.

Mark advanced to assistant crew leader at his job and his boss, Dennis, would spend a lot of time talking to him about the things of God. In the process, the Lord grabbed hold of Mark's heart and he gave his life to Jesus.

Mark got married in 1982 and today he and his wife have six beautiful children who are all serving the Lord. In 1984 Mark sensed a call on his life so he started volunteering at the Teen Challenge Center in Buffalo, NY where he lived. After over 25 years of involvement in Teen Challenge ministry Mark currently serves as the Executive Director of Heart of America Teen Challenge of Greater Kansas City. Mark also serves as the pastor of a church in Baldwin City, KS. Because of his ministry in the motorcycle club many Bikers attend the church where he pastors. Mark and his fellow Bikers (Barbarian Brotherhood Motorcycle Club) have ridden across the entire Nation, going from town to town raising money for Teen Challenge in their annual Ride for Freedom sharing the gospel with many they encounter. Over his years in the ministry, Mark has seen many people come to the Lord and be filled with the Holy Spirit.

Mark's faith has been challenged many times. He shared one story with me which was a true test. When his 4th son contracted bacterial meningitis the doctor told him that he never saw such a severe case. Mark knew that only a miracle could save him. A friend who had lost a daughter to the disease had a particularly strong burden to pray. He came to the hospital every day to intercede for this little boy. God heard and totally healed him. Mark's son didn't even have any sign of brain damage. Many children who have this disease do and the severity of this illness could have devastated Mark's son's brain. This was truly a miracle indeed.

Mark shared how the Lord had performed many miracles throughout his life but to share them all here would take too long. Mark's love for God and others keeps him constantly going.

Chapter 21

Grant Gomez

Isaiah 10: 27 – It shall come to pass in that day That his burden will be taken away from your shoulder, And his yoke from your neck, And the yoke will be destroyed because of the anointing oil.

Grant Gomez was born in 1958 in Washington State. His father was stationed in Tacoma, WA during his time in the armed forces. After his enlistment was up, their family moved back to Florida where Grant spent most of his life. On his father's side Grant's grandmother was half Creek Indian and his grandfather was half Mexican. His mother's family is of English and Welsh descent. His father was in the construction/excavation business and he also broke and trained horses. Grant was familiar with all of this as he worked with cattle and horses as a cowboy, as well as operating heavy equipment. He was raised to know who God was and he knew about the virgin birth of Jesus, but he didn't have a personal relationship with Him.

As a young boy, Grant was molested by a family member. This caused him great emotional harm and a deep anger and bitterness welled up inside him. He began to drink and do drugs at the age of 12. He was constantly in trouble and arrested several times. In 1977, Grant married Freda, his high school sweetheart. Because of his continual drinking their marriage was rocky and there were several separations over the years. In the mean time three daughters were born to them.

When Grant was 30 years old, God began moving in his life. He was invited to church where he heard the gospel for the first time. He eagerly fled to the cross where he was radically saved and set free. He never touched alcohol or drugs again. His new birth took place November 27, 1988. Grant described it like "God pulling all of the poison out of him." Because of the drastic change in Grant, Freda began to desire what she saw in him and within a year she too gave her life to the Lord. God began to heal and restore their marriage and in 1989 another daughter was born. Freda has experienced much healing too as she was set free from a lot of phobias and fears she had incurred during the early years of their marriage when Grant was still drinking. Their family is a miracle of restoration. All their daughters and sons-in-law serve the Lord faithfully. In 2009, Grant and Freda were blessed with a grandson.

In 1990, Grant began doing outreaches through his church. He developed a heart for people who were in bondage and began to lead them to Jesus. He also taught a vacation Bible school for 9 to 12-year-olds. Amazingly 22 of them received Christ as their personal Savior.

Grant began to sense the call to preach. His uncle who was a spirit-filled pastor told him that he needed the infilling of the Holy Spirit. At the time Grant wasn't in a church which believed in the Gifts of the Holy Spirit so he started going to a Full Gospel church. He received the Baptism of the Holy Spirit and after that he began to see many healings and miracles.

In 1992, Grant started a street ministry and saw God move mightily. He ministered to Hispanic people in migrant camps and also the Seminole Indians. He also visited the sick in hospitals and inmates in the prisons as well as ministered to the poor through food and clothing giveaways.

In the spring of 1993 an Australian Evangelist came to minister at Grant's mother-in-law's church. His name was Chris Harvey. At this time Grant visited this revival. He was hungry and desperate for more of God. At one of the meetings Grant was struck by the power of God and fire blazed through his soul. He understood what John the Baptist meant when he said in **Matthew 3:11b:** "He will baptize you with the Holy Spirit and fire." Just as the Apostles and Disciples were, Grant was drunk with the Holy Spirit and to this day His awesome presence has never left him. His ministry logo is "NO HIGH LIKE THE MOST HIGH."

Since that time, Grant has done healing conferences and revival meetings. Grant was ordained in 1998. He also pastored a church for 10 years before being called full time to travel along with his wife to preach revivals everywhere. "Freda is my best friend," Grant told me. "She has discernment and an administrative gift and I wouldn't be able to do what I do without her. She is always by my side wherever I go." Together they have a heart and call to Native Americans and have ministered to the Lakota in South Dakota on several Reservations.

Grant has also planted several churches in Florida and Texas as well as on an Indian reservation in Montana. In 2010 he was given a native-American flute which he plays at all his meetings and revivals. One lady was healed through listening to the pure melody of the instrument. He began making flutes in 2013 and has produced over 200. Grant also makes native-American jewelry. He has recorded 7 live worship music CDs and over 20 teaching CDs as well as writing two books. All of these help bring in the money needed for his ministry.

Grant's ministry is also a covering to a number of churches across the nation and has ordained 22 people into full time ministry. He hasn't had any formal education but has done a deep study of the Bible on his own for many years. He depends on God to guide him and the Holy Spirit to teach him as he remains in the Word.

Grant's faith was severely tested when on March 1, 2010 he was stricken with a stroke which left him partially paralyzed. He had booked some revival meetings in Texas so asked Freda to call the pastors there and have them cancelled. When she called, the pastors would hear none of it. They said to Grant that God was going to heal him and that he would be there for the meetings. So Grant and Freda packed up and went when the time arrived. Grant's mind had been affected by the stroke and he had a lot of difficulty putting thoughts into words. How was he going to get up there in the pulpit and preach? When he finally got up there to minister, all he could think of to say was "Jesus." The moment that word came out of his mouth, the Holy Spirit fell mightily on him. He was immediately healed and it was as though he had never had a stroke. Words of wisdom and power gushed from Grant as he preached an anointed message and the place was filled with God's majesty.

Grant portrays the love and power of God. As I interviewed him for this testimony I had the feeling that he had known me all of his life. I even had the opportunity to share with him a little bit of my testimony as well.

Chapter 22

Rick Scarborough

Matthew 5:13-16 - "You are the salt of the earth; but if the salt loses its flavor, how shall it be seasoned? It is then good for nothing but to be thrown out and trampled underfoot by men. You are the light of the world. A city that is set on a hill cannot be hidden. Nor do they light a lamp and put it under a basket, but on a lamp stand, and it gives light to all who are in the house. Let your light so shine before men, that they may see your good works and glorify your Father in heaven."

Rick was born in March of 1950 in Houston, TX. He describes his childhood as being one like Theodore Cleaver with a Godly mother and a father who worked for Sheffield Steel Plant. This plant had been started by his grandfather. Although his father didn't want anything to do with the church, Rick's mother was a Christian and took him to church regularly. She and a Sunday school teacher led Rick to a saving knowledge of Jesus Christ when he was 7 years old. By the age of 9 he felt a call on his heart to preach the gospel. But by the time he was in high school he began to drift away and imitate his father's secular world view.

Rick was very athletic and excelled in football. He gained a scholarship and went on to college in East Texas where he was rewarded a letter in his freshman year, a very rare accomplishment for someone in their first year. Around this time, God brought Mark Johnston into Rick's life. He was involved with Fellowship of Christian Athletes and God used him to bring Rick back on track with the Lord. During his sophomore year, he got involved with FCA and started sharing his testimony everywhere.

At his church, Rick was asked by the pastor to be a Youth Pastor. God's calling from years earlier burned in his heart so he accepted. Because of his obedience, the Lord opened more doors to him. He spent two years working in this capacity and one summer was brought in full time at a church. His double major was in political science and speech. After graduating he went on to seminary for two more years to obtain a master's degree.

Rick began pastoring at a small rural church where he baptized over 100 people. God expanded his vision and he stepped out in faith into newer pastures. He resigned his position at the church to buy a travel trailer and preach the gospel as an evangelist all over America. He conducted revivals full time for 14 years and went all over the world. He even preached for Mark Buntain in India. Over all he ministered in over 500 crusades until he settled down once more in a church of 1000 people. Under Mark's ministry he saw the church thrive. After that God called him to conduct a crusade.

Then Rick's life took a radical turn, one that would shake the community and even the nation. It began when he was invited to attend a high school assembly where he listened to a radical leftist speaker who promoted an illicit sex curriculum. He got into a discussion with her, refuting her claims that condoms are successful 94% of the time. Rick argued that even if condoms protect a person 94% of the time, why would anyone want to risk it? To illustrate this, Rick had challenged the speaker with, "Can you imagine an airline running an ad campaign that announces excitedly that only six out of every one hundred of their passengers who fly their airline die in a crash?" By now you have probably guessed it. The airline would be woefully lacking in passengers. Rick recorded the entire message and because it was legal in Texas to do so, he shared the message to his congregation. Later he went before the school board to express his reasons why he believed the sex education being presented was harmful to the students. The news caught on through the media and soon the nation was on fire about what was going on in Pearland. TX. Because of all the static, the principal who had allowed this was fired and was soon replaced by a new one. Another assembly was called and an entirely different message was given. A video was shown in which an ex-homosexual turned Christian shared the dangers of sex before marriage. He warned the students how illicit sex could lead to A.I.D.S.

The sex education curriculum at Pearland High School has since promoted abstinence until marriage. The Federal Drug Administration also has come out with a report of evidence that the A.I.D.S. virus is so small it can easily pass through a condom.

Rick has had a great impact on his church in Pearland. In his heated desire to call the nation back to Biblical morality, he has challenged his congregation to get involved in civic affairs. They heeded his advice and within two years, four members were elected to the school board.

Rick has had a mighty impact on the Pearland Ministerial Alliance as well. Because of his influence, the Alliance became involved in the city's affairs along with the National Day of Prayer. Pastors from different churches began to join together to exalt Jesus in the community. Although they maintained their individual doctrines and beliefs, their love for one another brought down a revival that literally changed the city of Pearland.

After involving about 25 pastors in Pearland in civic affairs, Rick began traveling the country to mobilize around 12,000 more pastors. Today he speaks all over the nation imploring people to get involved in political action in order to turn the country back to God.

In 2004, Rick and his family were immersed in grief when one of their daughters succumbed to a 7 year illness. Her memory brings them joy though as she had a strong faith in Christ. She was an award-winning athlete in track, having run many races. Rick says that her life and death has had a major impact on the family.

Chapter 23

B. Chad Connelly

Psalm 11:3 – If the foundations are destroyed, What can the righteous do?

Chad was born into a Christian family with deep conservative roots. He lived in a small community and attended a country church. He also attended Clemson University where he joined Army ROTC. This was a few years after the Vietnam War and because of the unpopularity of this engagement he and his fellow cadets were sometimes booed on campus. Because of President Reagan's positive influence on the culture, attitudes began to change and the "boos" eventually turned into cheers.

Chad met Michelle while attending college and they were married three years after graduation. Soon the couple got involved in local politics as volunteers. Chad began working for PSI, a national engineering consulting firm and quickly worked his way up to a Senior Management level running their operations across SC. Later he started his own business and encouraged others to start businesses of their own. His business grew nationally and even internationally.

Chad's growing concern for the nation and education drove him to do something about it around 2002. His spirit was grieved over the fact that children weren't being taught the truth about our national Christian heritage. Charlie "Tremendous" Jones, a national Christian speaker and author and a mentor to Chad, encouraged Chad to follow his passion for our nation. So Chad wrote a book called FREEDOM TIDE that has sold over 55,000 copies. He began speaking all over the nation and in some international countries about the true history of our Christian foundation and how our nation actually started on biblical truths.

Several years later, Chad was met with tragedy. His wife who had been suffering from depression lost her mother. This exasperated her depression and she became so distraught that she took her own life.

Chad was left with two small sons. The next two or three months were filled with heartache and indescribable loneliness. His two sons didn't understand it and they had a very difficult time dealing with it. "You never get over a suicide. You just get through it," Chad explained. "You have to move on." A buddy tried to encourage him during this time. He wanted him to meet a girl he knew but Chad wasn't ready so he just kept loving on him and encouraging him. One day Chad realized he had to do something to get himself moving again. He sat down and started writing out a list of blessings. When he was finished he realized he had put down on paper a total of 103 things he was thankful for. On New Year's Eve, Chad took off his wedding ring which he had never removed in over 18 years of marriage to Michelle. It was time to move on. At a meeting in January, his buddy once again asked him to meet this girl. Chad finally relented and in late January he met Dana, a widow who also was a victim of a suicide. She was left with two daughters. It wasn't long when Chad knew that God had put them together and six months later, they married. They prayed that God would give them a heart for one another and they would be able to emotionally release their dead spouses.

In 2011 Chad ran for RNC state party chairman and won. He came face to face with some who opposed his position on God and country but he met some Christians as well who supported his views. Reince Priebus, the Chairman of the Republican National Committee, was one of these people who befriended him and they often prayed together. Chad shared with me the reason Obama won a second term in 2008. It was because millions of Evangelical Christians stayed home instead of getting out to the polls. Chad ran for a second term as party chairman in 2013 and again won. In the mean time, Chairman Priebus had been working on him to be involved in the faith outreach team. Because it meant that he would have to move with his family to Washington DC, Chad had turned it down. Finally Reince told him that if he accepted the job, he could stay where he was. After praying about it with his wife, Chad accepted. Soon he began speaking to pastors about getting involved in the political process. Often pastors resisted the idea so Chad explained that registering people to vote and addressing the culture in a Biblical way is spiritual, not political. So far Chad has visited 33 states and personally spoken to over 35,000 pastors and faith leaders in an effort to get pastors and their churches involved. He understands that the political climate is affected by the spiritual one.

Chad ended his conversation with me by expressing his excitement about what God is doing and how He is continuing to lead him in this venture.

Chapter 24

Leon Brech

Psalm 91:11-12 – For He shall give His angels charge over you, to keep you in all your ways. In their hands they shall bear you up, lest you dash your foot against a stone.

Leon was born in Mitchell, SD and raised on a farm. He was fortunate enough to belong to a family where his parents made sure he was trained up in the way God wanted him to go. Because of his involvement in church and Sunday school, he had a distinct relationship with Jesus as early as he could remember. After he graduated from high school, he farmed until 1980 but his experiences as a farmer weren't always easy. Leon recalled the years of drought in the 1970s when the crops dried up for lack of rain.

Later on Leon moved to Florida and got involved in the choir there. He also became an elder as well as an usher in the church there. In 1990, he moved to Harrisburg, SD and lived there until 2010. When his marriage broke up, he rented out the house and moved again. Two years later he remarried.

Leon was a man of many skills. He not only was a farmer during his life but he also sold insurance in 1981 to the present day. He also ran the sound system in the church he attended after moving back from Florida.

One day Leon was to have an experience that literally shook his world. On June 18, 2014, he and a friend were working in the house in Harrisburg. This friend had called Leon to come help light a gas water heater in the basement. When the pair had walked into the house, the smell of propane wafted throughout the dwelling. They immediately opened all the doors and windows to air it out. As the men knelt down by the water heater to work on it there was a blast that shook the entire house. It was so severe the house was literally blown off its foundation and the garage was in shambles. Walls were blown out or cracked and destroyed as well as windows throughout the house. Leon doesn't remember how he and his friend got out of the house but the next thing he could recall was that they were standing on the front deck. Leon assumed that they had walked out of the utility room, went up the stairs and down the hall to the front door which led to the deck. Later on when the insurance adjuster came to look at the house, he said the stairs leading up from the basement were so badly damaged there was no way they could have supported the weight of the men. There had to have been another way they could have escaped but how? It was then that Leon realized God must have sent an angel to carry the men out to safety. A fireman who had rushed to the scene told Leon that he and his friend should have been blown up along with the house. There was also a 250 gallon fuel tank near the water heater that could have exploded but didn't. Leon and his friend incurred severe burns on their bodies and were flown by jet to the burn center in St Paul, MN. Leon's face was swollen beyond recognition but today he has no scars on his face. His arms were left scarred however which is a reminder to Leon of what God had done. The doctor at the burn center told Leon he would be there for at least six weeks. Due to the many prayers of the people in his church back home, he was discharged only two and a half weeks later. On July 4 Leon returned home and attended church the following Sunday. When I interviewed Leon he was in the process of putting a DVD together with photos of his experience as a testimony of what God has done for him. Leon wants people to know that God is for real and He is there waiting for them to come to Him.

Chapter 25

Chris Updegraff

Matthew 4:19–20 – And He said to them, "Follow Me, and I will make you fishers of men." They immediately left their nets and followed Him.

Chris was born in Monterey, CA in 1975. When he was two years old he moved with his parents to Salinas, CA where they settled on a half acre of land at the edge of town. Bonnie, Chris's mother, stayed at home and Ron, Chris's father, was kept busy with his janitorial business. The days were filled with exploration in the back yard creek, yellow dump trucks in the sand box, and "cowboys and Indians." Life as Chris knew it was good. In 1979 Chris's sister was born and "truth be told" he wasn't very happy about having to share his parents with a sibling.

By the time Chris was 5 years old, things took a turn in his life. His parents began to quarrel so his mother took him and his sister one night and left. From now on Chris would begin a journey of stress and upheaval as his white picket fence was no longer. The next place he would know as home was a shelter. It was a place of despair and Chris's eyes welled up in tears as he recalled this time in his life. After several months of this, his mother moved back home.

Though never divorcing, Chris's parents were legally separated. His mother went to work but trying to raise two children and keeping up with the house payments proved to be too much. She sought help at her church but instead of helping the family stay in their home, someone offered to buy the house. Because of being diagnosed with a mental illness Chris's father wasn't able to follow the profession he had been trained for. He took work as he could find it but eventually he was forced to live out of his van. He finally got a job cleaning a church. Chris grew bitter against Christians because he saw his father being left homeless with nowhere to go. More and more Chris felt like nobody cared and if he was going to make it he would have to do it on his own without the help of others.

At thirteen years of age, Chris lived in an apartment with his mother and on weekends they would visit his father. By now Ron was working and living in a small one room apartment. Though his father was back on his feet, Chris longed for the thing every child of separated parents wants – to see his parents get back together. Then one day…they did! Chris rejoiced inside. His father had changed and he loved his mother unconditionally. The joy Chris felt was only temporary however.

The area of Salinas Chris had moved to was filled with Mexican gangs. One time he was beaten up and the bike he had built was stolen. The situation at school with gang members threatening Chris grew worse and when his mother complained to the principal she was told that nothing could be done about it. Finally, in a last ditch effort, his parents shipped him off to South Dakota to live with an aunt. It was the only option at the time so at age 17, Chris would begin a new journey in Brandon, SD, where he attended Brandon Valley High School. The routine of a normal family and school life began and for the first time since he was 5 years old he felt like he could relax a little. He felt safe. The summer of Chris's senior year in high school, his parents and sister moved here from California.

After graduation, Chris went to a technical school in Wyoming where he learned auto mechanics. After graduating, he began a job at a car dealer. It was rough at first because he was having a very difficult time fixing a car. He decided to quit until his manager talked him into coming back. Chris felt that his boss had given him permission to fail and this set him free from his fear of not being able to achieve. From then on he excelled at what he did until he advanced to being a top mechanic.

Chris wasn't following the Lord at this time and he spent his weekends drinking and partying with friends. He would go with them to race their cars around the loop downtown. This was where he met Mariah whom he would marry within a year. In order to be married in the church they had to take premarital counseling. After they were married they never went to church and Chris continued his walk away from the Lord. Empty and unfulfilled in life Chris began taking an interest in other women and an affair ensued. Having set Chris apart, God still had a hold on him and He spoke to his spirit, "Chris, what are you doing?" Guilt plagued him so badly he finally confessed his infidelity to Mariah. After this Mariah didn't want anything to do with him even after Chris agreed to go with her to marriage counseling. Then things began to take a turn.

Mariah went to hear a speaker at church on Sunday and she came away saved and filled with the Holy Spirit. In spite of all this Mariah still wanted a divorce. In desperation, Chris tried everything to win her back. Nothing worked. One snowy Sunday, Chris felt so hopeless that he no longer cared if he lived or died. Driving on an old snow covered highway, he pressed his foot down on the accelerator until he was going 105 miles per hour. Then a voice began speaking to his spirit. "Follow me!" Chris asked God if He was going to bring Mariah back to him but the voice only said, "Follow me!" Chris never got the answer he so badly desired but he made a decision then and there to follow Christ. When Chris took that unconditional step of faith, God answered the desires of his heart and soon Mariah came home. Through counseling they worked through many of their problems and today they minister together to others who are struggling in their marriages.

One day God brought a challenge to Chris and Mariah which shook their faith. Chris felt the call to go to the Middle East with a man who went there often to rescue Christian people, mainly children and young women, out of slavery. At first Mariah was terrified with the idea because she didn't want to see Chris being put in such danger. After praying about it for a year and a half, however, she released her husband to go. So Chris contacted the man and made plans to go with him on the next trip. After raising the money to go, circumstances arose forcing the trip to be postponed. This went on for a year until Chris was finally able to make the trip. It was a success as he and the man who had set things up were able to rescue 179 people. 89 others walked off the slave fields. They managed this by purchasing these people for as little as $24 per person.

Today Chris waits for God's next assignment. He told me he is miserable unless he is following the Lord's leading in his life.

Chapter 26

Kurt and Gina Schiferl

Luke 14:10 - Likewise, I say to you, there is joy in the presence of the angels of God over one sinner who repents.

Kurt and Gina came from similar backgrounds in which neither had heard that they could have a personal relationship with Jesus Christ. When Gina's mother attended a women's coffee Bible study, she heard it for the first time. Gina remembers that day when her mother came home and was all lit up because she had received the good news that Jesus had died on the cross for her. Immediately she lined Gina and her siblings up and began sharing the plan of salvation with them. All but one received Jesus into their hearts that day. Gina was lit on fire for the Lord and she got involved in a Bible study with other middle school and high school students. It was led by a DJ who had begun it. There were 40 - 60 kids who crowded in different homes every Monday night. All were aglow and eager to learn more about Jesus. When Gina graduated from High School her vigor waned and she began to slip away from the things of God.

Kurt and Gina met while at college and got married shortly after they graduated. When they moved to another town, they met a couple who first introduced them to a higher step of faith. One time they were invited to a special service at this couple's church and Kurt was baffled by the informality of it all. He had been used to a very conventional structured church service. So that was the only time they attended that church. However, God had something prepared for the Schiferls in years to come, something that would forever change their lives.

The Schiferls moved yet again and they got involved with the party crowd where there was no shortage of smoking and drinking. In the meantime they had two children - first a daughter and then 11 months later an unplanned son. It was a blessing in disguise because Gina couldn't have any more children. Had the Schiferls waited to have another child as they had planned, Caleb would never have been born. This son has been a great blessing to them.

As Gina cared for these little ones and worked full time she began to sink into a deep clinical depression and was taking up to five different medications for it. It seemed like the cloud would never be removed from her life until a lady invited her to a Women's Aglow Meeting. Gina remembers what the speaker shared that day in detail. She spoke about the Israelites crossing the Jordan River and how they picked up stones to use to build an altar on the other side. The story so touched Gina's heart that she realized she needed the Lord and gave her life back Him. She then took her children and started attending a tiny little church that was filled with godly people who demonstrated the power and love of Christ. At that time Kurt was away at guard camp. When Gina poured out her heart about what God had done over the phone to him, she received a cold reception. This left Gina feeling disappointed and she sensed an inner warning to move slowly ahead with Kurt concerning her spiritual experience. Gina wasn't able to hold it inside, however, and it just kept bubbling out to Kurt until one day on the road, Kurt lashed out in profanity at Gina and accused her of being a religious fanatic. Eventually he finally agreed to attend the little spirit- filled church she had been going to but he insisted on a list of conditions. When he got there, he discovered the conditions weren't necessary, and instead, he sensed only the love of Christ emanating from the people. For a while the Schiferls attended both the denomination they were raised in and the little church they felt God's presence in until they eventually began going there exclusively. Their lives were so changed that their old friends stopped inviting them to their drinking parties even though the Schiferls never said anything to them about it. Their former friends just seemed to sense a change that convicted them.

Gina developed fibromyalgia which began to have a major effect on her body and she was in a lot of pain. She went up for prayer regularly for this and the depression she had struggled with for so long. Through persistent prayer, she was gradually healed of both of these things. Gina told me that she believes that God heals in many ways. Sometimes it is instantaneously. Sometimes it is gradually and other times God will use doctors and medication. Still other times God chooses to call people home to be with Him where they will have brand new perfect bodies with no more pain and suffering. Gina describes her healing as miraculous.

Kurt and Gina shared stunning miracles with me, two of which I will share here.

One time Kurt's National Guard unit was sent to Panama for a special project. He was operating a JD-410 Backhoe and was on his way down a very steep mountain when it broke loose and was headed towards a cliff with a big drop off. There was nothing to stop the backhoe from its deadly plunge. Then suddenly it was like a hand came out of nowhere and jerked the machine back, turned the front end around, and set it down so it lay safely on the road away from the cliff's edge. Unbeknownst to Kurt, at the same moment Gina had been praying back home for him. "A dire urgency to pray for Kurt fell upon me," Gina expressed. "I shut my office door, got on my knees and I cried out to God and yet I didn't really know what for. I only sensed Kurt was in some kind of danger." They believe that God had sent an angel to hold the backhoe from going over the cliff that day.

Another time, their daughter injured herself at church. The toenail on her right foot was nearly torn off and lifted up at a 90 degree angle. Gina didn't know what to do so she prayed in the spirit with others for her daughter. After a few minutes they looked down at the foot to discover it had been completely healed. The toenail had lain back down and it never got black or fell off in the days to come. Shortly after that, they couldn't even tell which foot had the injured toenail. God used this to increase Gina's faith and to prepare her to pray for others to be healed. She knows that if God can heal a little girl's toenail, then He can heal even more significant things.

Today Kurt works as a commissioned minister for Volunteers of America. They serve many people including the poor in all kinds of practical ways. Kurt, as a spirit filled Christian, has many opportunities to share his faith with others there. I was surprised to find out that the Volunteers of America was founded by the son of William Booth. His name is familiar to many because he started the Salvation Army.

Kurt loves children and always is anxious to join the children in children's church as a helper. Gina prefers working with women and has served as a women's ministry leader, adult Sunday school teacher, and an event speaker. Together they are being mightily used by the Lord.

Chapter 27

Carla Noe

Philippians 1: 6 – For I am confident of this very thing, that He who began a good work in you will perfect it until the day of Christ Jesus.

Carla made a decision to follow Jesus when she was ten years old. But her heart was stony ground because she wasn't rooted in the word of God and her new faith withered away. She had little support at home and her parents quarreled all the time because her mother wanted to take Carla and her siblings to church and her father didn't want her to attend church. For some unknown reason the Bible was never read at home where Carla grew up. As a result she got off to a bad start with the Lord and, as a teenager, she backslid completely. Being a typical teen she wanted to fit in with the crowd so she became a follower rather than a leader. She didn't go along with everything her friends did, however, and she attributes it to the fact that she didn't fit in well enough to be trusted and her mother and sisters prayed for her.

After graduating from high school, Carla immediately got married to a man she didn't love as an escape from her parents' house and also because it seemed like a good thing to do. After all, her friends were getting married and she didn't want to be left out of the equation. As a result, Carla mistreated her husband and she regrets it to this day. "He didn't deserve the way I acted towards him," she remarked.

On February of 1978, Carla married her current husband, Joe, and their only child was born on January 28 the following year. The couple was young and immature and always had itchy feet for something better. So they moved five times in four years until they finally ended up in Billings, MT where Joe went to a technical school to be an auto mechanic. On the last day of school he helped someone lift their toolbox and ended up injuring a disk in his lower back. He wound up having a laminectomy.

This incident resulted in Joe's heart softening towards God. The Lord was doing a work in Carla's heart as well.

Carla was working at Church's Chicken where a Baptist preacher would often come. Every time he was leaving he would go out the door singing, "Are You Ready for the Judgment?" This convicted Carla but she was afraid to ask him why he would sing it. She knew what the answer would be. Carla and Joe began to watch Jimmy Swaggart on television on Sunday morning while Joe was recovering from his back surgery.

One Sunday morning in August 1983 they were watching when the altar call was given. Carla was crying as the Holy Spirit drew her powerfully towards Jesus. Joe said to her, "I am going to do this. Will you do this with me?" The couple knelt down right in the middle of their tiny living room and cried out in repentance, asking Jesus to come in and take over their lives. Carla expressed, "I never felt so clean and new!" They began attending a church in Billings, got involved in a ministry and began to grow.

A couple of years later Lowell Lundstrom visited the church and shared about Trinity Bible College. Joe wanted to go and Carla agreed to go. They sold most of their things and moved to Ellendale where Carla got her teaching degree along with the Biblical Studies degree.

The couple moved a few times before finally settling in Sioux Falls in 2005. Throughout these years Carla learned to forgive her earthly father and trust her heavenly Father. As a result she was able to send a letter to her father which shared the love of God with him. His heart was broken and he decided to entrust the rest of his live to Jesus. A huge change came over him and Carla's mother reconciled with him after that. Carla knows that she will meet him again someday in Heaven.

Carla became a licensed pastor with the church and today she is involved with Aglow Prison Ministries in South Dakota. On occasion she even gets the opportunity to preach at the prison in Pierre. Although she wasn't open to prison ministry in the beginning, she is glad that she obeyed the Holy Spirit to do this.

In 2010 Carla started to ache all over her body. It got so bad that she couldn't stand to have anyone touch her. When she went to the doctor, he told her that she had fibromyalgia. She had to take a lot of medication that made her sleepy. This was devastating because it interfered with her ministry as well as her everyday life. In desperation she asked for prayer one night when she attended her weekly small group at church. As soon as the group of people prayed and laid hands on her, Carla felt what she described as a cold sensation sweep from the top of her head to the soles of her feet. Every ounce of pain left her body and hasn't returned since. Carla has been able to throw away all her medication.

Chapter 28

Todd Schlekeway

I Timothy 4:12 – Let no one despise your youth, but be an example to the believers in word, in conduct, in love, in spirit, in faith, in purity.

Todd was born in Valentine, NE to godly parents who were teachers at Mission, SD on the Rosebud Sioux Indian Reservation. His maternal grandparents were shining lights for Christ who set an example for the family to follow. Todd accepted Christ at a Bible camp when he was very young.

The family moved to Mobridge, SD where Todd attended grade school, middle school and high school. He was very active in sports, especially basketball, and his father was his high school coach. After graduation, Todd attended college at Northern State University in Aberdeen, SD and the University of Sioux Falls in Sioux Falls, SD where he continued his basketball career. Todd became involved in the Fellowship of Christian Athletes organization during his time as a student-athlete at the University of Sioux Falls.

Todd told me that there have been two spheres of influence in his life – sports and politics. As a leader in the Fellowship of Christian Athletes he was able to be a strong Christian example to the high school students at Lincoln High School. Todd has always attempted to live by the instruction Paul gave to Timothy in **I Timothy 4:12** and he taught the students to live the same way. "People are watching you," Todd would remark. He would never allow the students to use their youth as an excuse to not be their best for Christ.

Todd has also been drawn by God to be involved in politics. He served in the state legislature in both the House and the Senate and was able to let his light for Jesus shine there. Todd shared that there are a lot of Christians serving in the South Dakota legislature and every week during the session he attended a Bible study where the room was always full.

He specifically pointed out to me that that he has an admiration for South Dakota Representative Roger Hunt and United States Senator John Thune for their strong godly convictions. "When I served in the legislature there were some issues that I could compromise on," Todd said, "but never on social issues involving my Biblical moral values." He stresses that believers need to practice **I Timothy 2:1-4** by praying for their elected officials that they would make biblical decisions in leading the country. A biblical world view is essential to getting the country back on track according to the founding fathers.

Right now Todd is working in the telecommunications industry and travels extensively throughout the country. He hopes to return to elective office in the future when the timing is right. Todd told me that these experiences he has had in sports and politics has caused him to grow in his relationship with Jesus.

Today, Todd is married to Jill and they have two sons, Gavin and Grant. At this writing they are expecting another son this summer. He is raising his children the same way he was brought up by instilling in them the importance of knowing Jesus and following Him.

In closing, Todd emphasized that as a Christian, his identity isn't wrapped up in anything he does, but it is connected to Christ. The other thing he stresses is that he can't put his faith in man but only in Jesus.

Chapter 29

Tony Perkins

Acts 5:29 – Peter and the other apostles answered and said, "We ought to obey God rather than men."

Tony was born in a small community called Sharonville, Ohio just outside Cincinnati. He was the oldest of four children. At this time his parents weren't believers but when Tony was five years old he had the opportunity to attend a small church with a congregation of only 75. He enjoyed it so much that he asked his father to take him back there. When he did, before his father could stop him, Tony ran right up to the front row as fast as his little legs could carry him and sat down to hear what the pastor had to say. Of course his father then had to follow suit. When the pastor began to preach it was as though he was speaking directly to Tony's father. The next day the pastor visited Tony's parents in their home and led them both to a saving knowledge of Jesus Christ. At the age of nine, Tony decided to follow Jesus as well. He never wavered from his faith from then on.

Tony joined the Marine Corps upon graduating from high school. By this time his parents had moved to Louisiana and after his stint in the service, Tony joined them there. He began to work for the sheriff's office and later went to LSU. In 1982 he went on an outreach to New Mexico through his church and this was where he met his wife, Lawana. He invited her to go with him for a bike ride on a bicycle built for two. 24 hours later he felt that Lawana was to become his wife and two and a half years later, they were married. Today they have five children – the oldest being 23 years old and the youngest 7.

Tony's heart's desire was to be a policeman and a preacher and throughout his life he did both. In fact at the young age of 15 he started preaching in nursing homes to the patients there. The last thing he ever wanted to do was be involved in politics. But when he surrendered to full time ministry in 1992, God led him to be involved in the government.

In 1995, after much prayer, Tony ran for the LA legislature and won easily. He served only two terms because he felt he should term limit himself. While he served there, he worked on family policy issues and helped get healthy bills passed. When his term was up he was encouraged to run for the Insurance Commissioner position but then a turn of events ensued. Dr. James Dobson approached Tony to ask him to become president of the Family Research Council.

At the time he got involved in the FRC Tony never realized that the country would sink to such a point that Christians were in danger of losing their religious freedoms.

"We have been called to glorify God and all that we do by following the example of the early disciples," Tony shared. "We are at this point in our nation today because in many ways the church is indistinguishable from the world. We are called to be salt and light by living out our faith on a daily basis."

"Right before God does something powerful these words so often precede it – Fear not!" Tony exclaimed. Right now he has been fighting for religious freedom at the Supreme Court level. The Justices have been challenged with statements such as "Marriage has been between one man and one woman for 5,000 years. Why should we change it after only ten years of arguments to the contrary?" Although Tony doesn't know which way the Supreme Court will go with this decision, he is cautiously optimistic that most on the Court will see the dangers in redefining marriage. Should marriage be redefined in our country, it would mean children would be indoctrinated in the ways of homosexuality in the schools, through TV, the media and Hollywood and parents wouldn't have any recourse.

"What should we do?" I asked Tony.

"Fathers need to engage their children, spend time with them and lead by example," he answered. "Pastors need to challenge their congregations from their pulpits to live out biblical truths in their daily lives and urge fathers to take leadership roles in their homes to raise their children with biblical values."

"Do you see any hope?" I inquired.

"People are beginning to become more aware of what is going on and the threats to their freedoms. This is what it will take to turn things around. People will seek out churches where biblical truths are being taught and start attending there," Tony assured. "And the solutions will never come through political leaders. These challenges are only something the church can control."

Tony agreed with me that groups like the Family Research Council are growing and they will continue to educate people with the truth and fight for religious freedom.

Today we are beginning to live with the results of the Supreme Court's decision to legalize same sex marriage in all 50 states. However we can take comfort in the fact that we have people like Tony Perkins fighting for us.

Chapter 30

Tracey Eberhard

Luke 14:23 – And the master said to the slave, "Go into the highways and along the hedges, and compel them to come in, so that my house may be filled."

Tracey was born in Long Beach, CA. Her father was a blind gospel pianist and was in a quartet that traveled from place to place to spread the gospel through their performances. Tracey's family was involved with several different gospel quartets, in several different churches and concerts. Unfortunately, not all members of those quartets set good Christian examples behind the scenes. Also Tracey's parents quarreled a lot at home and therefore didn't model how a true Christian should behave. Their marriage eventually ended in a divorce and years later each of them married believers who drew them to a closer relationship with Jesus. Because of her home life and the poor examples that some of the other gospel entertainers set Tracey struggled with Christianity.

Tracey married when she was only 17 years old and their first daughter was born shortly thereafter. Another daughter arrived almost two years later. It was shortly after that when Tracey became the victim of a violent crime. Her husband couldn't deal with what had happened, and turned to drinking and drugs. Tracey lost everything as a result – her marriage and her two daughters. Eventually, she went to live with an aunt and uncle and got a job.

Tracey underwent two major surgeries. As she was preparing to go into her second surgery, Tracey told God to take her life, or do something with it! Unbeknownst to her, her grandmother had been praying fervently for her. When Tracey woke up after her surgery she immediately began to pray and read her Bible. As she was praying she sought God's direction for her life. She was released from the hospital on Good Friday and went to church on Easter Sunday where she met Barry.

They began seeing one another and he discipled her so she learned how to live the Christian life. Barry had been praying for a wife and believed God wanted him to marry Tracey. He didn't ask her to marry him; he TOLD her she was going to be his wife. She got upset and told him "NO WAY!" She had had it with marriage and wanted no part of it. But Barry persisted so Tracey told him that he could meet her girls and if they didn't like him she wouldn't see him anymore. He agreed to this condition.

Barry had a plan. He decided that if he took her and the girls to Disneyland they would have to like him. So he and Tracey went to visit the girls. He rented a hotel room for himself and another room for Tracey and the girls. Barry loved children and soon he was playing with the girls in the pool and on the floor. He didn't even have to take them to Disneyland first for them to like him. They loved him right away. So Tracey asked God if Barry was His choice for her. He made it clear that he was, so they soon got married. In August of 2015 they will have been married 34 years.

Barry and Tracey haven't been able to have any children of their own but they thoroughly enjoy children especially their own six grandsons, the offspring of Tracey's girls.

Barry and Tracey lived in California for the first few years of their marriage. They moved to Colorado and lived there until they moved to South Dakota in 1996. They spent the majority of their time with Barry's parents. After his father passed away, Tracey began to seek the Lord about a ministry that she and Barry could be involved in together.

 It wasn't long when a friend invited them to go on a motorcycle ride with them (a dinner run) where after riding for a while they wound up at a restaurant to enjoy a meal together. Tracey always enjoyed riding behind Barry on his motorcycle, but the motorcycle was getting very old. These new friends introduced them to CMA (Christian Motorcyclists

Association) and Tracey felt drawn by the Lord to get involved with this group. Barry, however, drew back because he didn't like the stigma that was associated with bikers. The more Tracey prodded and pleaded with Barry to join CMA with her, the more he dug in his heels and wanted no part of it. Tracey prayed for over a year asking God to change Barry's heart towards this and to make it clear to him that He wanted them both involved in this ministry. She was also praying that God would supply them with a new bike. Then one day a miracle happened. A check came in the mail out of nowhere. It turned out that a great grandmother who had been gone for 30 years left her mineral rights to them. The check covered the down payment for the new motorcycle that Barry wanted. This was the incident that changed Barry's heart. He took it as a sign from God that they were to get involved in CMA. And the checks kept coming until the bike was paid off.

Tracey was elated and she and Barry soon got involved in prison ministry through CMA and the M2 program. They also helped with Bill Glass Weekend of Champions when it came to South Dakota. The entertainers and athletes would minister in the prison all weekend and CMA'ers were allowed to ride some of their bikes into the prison yards. So Barry took advantage of the opportunity and rode his motorcycle into one. About 2005, Tracey felt God was leading her to have her own motorcycle in order to reach the women bikers for Christ. Barry bought her one in 2008 and that year she was able to ride it into four different prison yards. For ten years, Tracey has coordinated the P-2 Project, a Jail Visitation Program at the Minnehaha County Jail. She interviews the inmates and sets them up with volunteers who visit them once a week. Tracey and Barry also do Bible studies for chemically dependent teens that are in a treatment program. Somebody anonymously has provided Bibles for the teens. This ministry has been both challenging and rewarding. They have met some of them back in jail. But others have come up to them and thanked them for what they have done for them.

One of the big events that Barry and Tracey are involved in every year is the Sturgis Bike Rally. "We help out in many practical ways and earn the right to share Christ with the people," Tracey told me. Right now they have been in charge of the court house parking lots. This has given them many opportunities to pray with people before and after their court sessions. One time Tracey met a lady in a restroom who had a great need. Tracey offered to pray for her and they were both blessed. "It was a divine appointment," Tracey said. She knew that God had led her to the right place at the right time.

This year Sturgis will celebrate the 75th anniversary of the Bike Rally. 1.3 million People are expected to attend. Barry and Tracey plan to be there for two weeks this summer.

Barry and Tracey started out as chapter members of CMA, then became Chapter officers and now they are part of the state leadership. They serve as Area Representatives for Eastern South Dakota. They always wear their biker vests because they let people know where they stand. It gives them many opportunities to share Christ with others. Tracey stressed to me that CMA is a ministry and not just a "burp and ride" group.

CMA has several different types of ministries, including Youth, Prison, etc. But, it's main ministry is to the Biking world. They also have many activities that enrich their members' lives and encourage them in the ministry God has called them to. They have annual celebrations for children, teens, and adults. One of the highlights is The Changing of the Colors Rally in October on Iron Mountain in Arkansas where people can go on rides to enjoy the scenery in between life-enriching seminars along with plenty of praise and worship and challenging messages.

CMA is celebrating their 40th anniversary this year. It started when a pastor wanted to gain a better relationship with his son by taking him on motorcycle rides. He began going to bike rallies where he volunteered in many practical ways such as helping to pick up trash and other mundane tasks. It eventually earned him the right to preach and have his own booth there and soon he was driving around on his bike, going to rallies everywhere and sharing the gospel as he went.

CMA International ministries have been established in over 30 countries around the world. CMA has partnered with 3 other ministries (Mission Ventures, Open Doors, and the Jesus Film Project). Millions of people have come to Christ and millions of Bibles have been smuggled into closed countries. The JESUS film is also being shown all over the world. Barry & Tracey feel very blessed that God has brought them into the ministry of CMA.

Chapter 31

Shantel Krebs

James 1:2-3 – My brethren, count it all joy when you fall into various trials, knowing that the testing of your faith produces patience.

Shantel was born in Arlington, SD - a 4th generation farm girl. She was fortunate in that her parents were hard working devout Christians who took her to church every Sunday. Her mother also took her to Bible studies and spent many hours volunteering in the community. Shantel helped out with this by the time she was in the 1st grade.

Not only did Shantel help others wherever she could in the small town, she worked very hard on the farm, cleaning up fallen trees around the farm yard, walking beans and riding her horse in the ditches while picking up trash. As industrious as she was, Shantel began her own lawn mowing business while in the 5th grade using an old push mower. She remembers visiting with her customers after mowing their yards. This caused a love to grow in her heart for the elderly and she spent many hours volunteering in a nursing home where she would sometimes arrive on horseback. "I have learned a lot from the elderly, by hearing about how they handled challenges encountered throughout their lives," Shantel remarked.

It has been the habit of Shantel to begin her day with morning walks as early as 5:00 AM when she prays and worships God. She likes to meditate on **Psalm 118:24** during this time as she sings out in praise, "This is the day the Lord has made; We will rejoice and be glad in it." She recognizes the importance of being thankful to God each day and she will talk to Him several times throughout her day.

As a much disciplined person, Shantel has started three businesses and this has prepared her for the office she serves in today. She first got involved in politics as a senior in high school when she served as a legislative page. She spent many hours volunteering in political campaigns and also served as Vice Chair for the Republican Party in her county and the state party. She served ten years in the state legislature in South Dakota. When someone approached her about the office of the South Dakota Secretary of State, she was encouraged to run for that position and was elected.

Shantel shared with me that she makes no decision without first seeking God for direction because she knows that everything she does has an effect on others. She purposely surrounds herself with hard-working, dedicated Christians so that she will stay focused on what is important. Her goal is to run her office as efficiently as possible in areas of business services and secure elections.

Shantel has come across a lot of great hard working, God loving individuals in Pierre who care for South Dakota and the nation. Christians serve not only in the legislature but in the every-day jobs that make government function more effectively.

Shantel has been married for 16 years to Mitch. This woman of God knows and has experienced the ups and downs of every-day life so she reflects on **Romans 5:3-5** which states, "And not only that, but we also glory in tribulations, knowing that tribulation produces perseverance; and perseverance, character; and character, hope. Now hope does not disappoint, because the love of God has been poured out in our hearts by the Holy Spirit who was given to us."

Chapter 32

Denae Baustian

Luke 15:4 – What man of you, having a hundred sheep, if he loses one of them, does not leave the ninety-nine in the wilderness, and go after the one which is lost until he finds it.

Denae was one of those lost sheep who, as a child, gave her heart to the Lord but then went out into the wilderness, totally lost until the Good Shepherd found her. Here is her story.

Denae was born in Sioux Falls in 1966. Her mother had known nothing but abuse when she grew up and so she didn't know how to love. As a result she was hurtful and demanding towards Denae. Like Cinderella Denae was forced to clean the house and cook before she was even old enough to go to school. She had to stand on a stool in order to reach the stove to cook meals for the family. She was expected to straighten the house thoroughly by moving every stick of furniture to clean under it. Every wall, every knick knack and everything had to be dusted and scrubbed flawlessly. Every article of clothing or linen had to be perfectly folded and neatly stacked in a drawer or cupboard. If it wasn't, Denae's mother would empty it all out on the floor and make her do it all over again. All this hard work coupled with sports caused Denae to grow very strong physically.

Denae was also terribly neglected when she wasn't being beaten. At the age of two or three, after she dressed and fed herself, she would wander the neighborhood alone. On one occasion two strange men picked her up in their van and after molesting her dumped her off in a strange neighborhood. Denae managed to find her way back home and her mother never knew what happened.

Denae loved the outdoors and would befriend the snakes and spiders. Oftentimes she would bring them home as pets. She would observe children going to school and she wanted to go too. Even though she was too young, she would often follow the other children and wind up in the classroom with them. After a couple of hours the teacher would come to the realization that Denae didn't belong there and send her home.

Denae's parents didn't get along so after 2 ½ years of marriage they got a divorce. Between the interim of the separation and remarrying, a baby sister arrived on the scene. Her mother treated her the opposite way she treated Denae. She pampered and spoiled her and this caused Denae to dislike her. When Denae was four years old, her parents divorced again. At that time they lived in Illinois but after the divorce, Denae, her sister and mother moved back to Sioux Falls. Because of her abusive situation, Denae strived to be perfect and she got straight A's in school. Her sister did poorly and didn't study but she wasn't punished for that as Denae would have been.

Denae was filled with anger and because of being mistreated she developed PTSD (post traumatic stress disorder) which caused her a lot of emotional and physical pain.

When Denae and her sister were removed from their home by the state, they went to live with a Christian couple who took them to church. Their mother was in a hospital to be treated for mental illness and when she was released the children were returned to her. Although she herself didn't go to church, Denae's mother wanted her and her sister to go so she arranged for a bus to pick them up each Sunday for children's church. Denae wanted to go so she would sit outside for hours waiting for the bus to come. In church she would run up, in tears, to the altar to give her life to the Lord just about every Sunday. She understood what salvation was about but had no concept of what making Jesus Lord of her life meant.

Because of the years of feeling unloved and unwanted, Denae lived an independent life, not trusting anyone. However she did get involved in sports and music. She played basketball but her mother never came to any of the games. She also played the clarinet so she would have to walk to school in the dark to make it to the practices. By the time she was twelve years old, she became sexually active and began getting involved with alcohol and drugs. At sixteen she decided she really wanted to follow Jesus so she gave that up and began listening to Christian music and making every effort to serve God. The sexual addiction had a strong grip on her life, though, so she was unable to give that up at the time. This didn't last long though. She met a man who liked to hang out in the bars and she would go along. Although she didn't do drugs any more, she would drink.

When Denae was 19, she met Paul Baustian who wasn't a believer. They lived together for a while and then decided to get married. When a pastor refused to marry them they went to a Justice of the Peace. Denae was trying to follow Jesus but she hadn't totally surrendered her life to Him. She didn't realize that she was building her life on shifting sand instead of solid rock. She did go to church, however, and talked Paul into going with her. After a year, Paul received Jesus into his heart. For a while things went pretty well. They built up their business and were thriving.

Then Denae joined the fire department where she was surrounded by men. She had to listen to their foul language and off-colored jokes but she felt they treated her better than many professing Christians. Paul wasn't very happy about this situation. Because of his own background, he was broken and unable to love Denae the way God wanted him to. Instead of treating her as Jesus would, he would selfishly force himself upon her until she could no longer tolerate it. Finally she moved out of the house and left their five children there for Paul to raise.

Denae got a job in a place where a video lottery machine was located. She began putting money into it. Because of the trauma of dealing with her childhood along with her troubled marriage, she lost herself in this new deadly habit. She poured her money into the machine until she began stealing money from the fire department to feed her habit. In the meantime the devil lied to her, telling her that her situation was hopeless and nobody would want her after what she did. She decided that there was nothing left for her to do but to end her life. Having worked as a paramedic, she scouted around the house for medications that she could take that would kill her and not just leave her as a vegetable. After looking for a while, she decided to wait until morning to make the deadly move. By morning, however, she thought about her children and changed her mind about suicide. Instead she thought it was time to confess to God, her husband and the authorities about what she had done. But by this time the police were onto her and they came to investigate. There was a period of a year of legal process also when Denae underwent extensive counseling and treatment as well as the 12 step program to free her of her gambling addiction. It was during this time she committed her life entirely to the Lord. By the time she was incarcerated she was able to take full responsibility for what she had done. She was ready to accept the consequences.

During her time in prison, Denae grew by leaps and bounds in her faith. She had plenty of time to study the Bible, pray, and journal everything the Holy Spirit was teaching her. The other prisoners would notice her as she prayed and opened the Word so some of them would come to her and ask for prayer. One lady, a confessed witch, opened up her heart to Denae and Denae listened to her. She never judged her or tried to convince her that she was wrong. Instead she loved her with the love of Jesus. The lady grew to respect her and a good relationship developed out of it. The day Denae left the prison, she spoke once more to this woman and told her that she wanted to see her in Heaven and that she would be praying for her to receive Jesus as her Personal Savior.

While Denae was in prison she and Paul's relationship was rocky and there were many months when they didn't speak to one another. Nine months before Denae's release, Paul visited her and told her that he was ready to totally commit himself to her as a loving husband. This happened in August 2014 and they have been dedicated to one another ever since. Denae says it is like being married all over again. She was released from prison right before Memorial Day 2015 and the couple continues to grow in the midst of their transformation.

Because God removed the deep seated anger from Denae's soul, she has been able to forgive her mother and love her with an agape love. She will read the Bible to her and pray for her. Although she hasn't seen a change in her, Denae believes God will transform her mother the same way He has changed her. Denae has a strong will that she believes God has given her in order to survive all the bad years. But instead of going her way, she allows the Holy Spirit to direct her path.

Chapter 33

Paul Baustian

James 5:19-20 – Brethren, if anyone among you wanders from the truth, and someone turns him back, let him know that he who turns a sinner from the error of his way will save a soul from death and cover a multitude of sins.

Paul was born in Luverne, Minnesota, the oldest of eight children. He was raised on a farm and was accustomed to hard work. His dad was demanding of his five boys. While they toiled outside, Paul's mother worked inside the house, cleaning and canning the string beans that Paul picked from the garden. At an early age, Paul earned money by selling pigs at the fair through 4H. He also did chores for other farmers. Although Paul always went to church with his family, he never knew the Lord in a personal way. He just went through the rituals until he began to feel they were a waste of his time. When he left home, he no longer went to church.

By the time Paul was fourteen years old, he began to get a taste of the world when he went to the Minnesota State Fair. He became wild and began drinking and doing drugs. When he was older, he would buy a 12 pack of beer and drink it every night. He also became addicted to sex. He loved to race his car up and down the streets at 120 miles an hour. Oftentimes he would be drinking as he was doing this and would wind up in a field not knowing how he got there. One time he smashed into a fence at high speeds and earned a concussion. It wasn't until later though that Paul realized that it was God who spared him.

You read more about his story in Denae's testimony but I will add this. Paul was born again when he received Jesus as his Personal Savior at the age of 29. He and Denae have five grown children and seven grandchildren, one of whom is waiting for them in Heaven.

Chapter 34

Jeff Kuper

Matthew 28:18-20 - And Jesus came and spoke to them, saying, "All authority has been given to Me in heaven and on earth. go therefore and make disciples of all the nations, baptizing them in the name of the Father and of the Son and of the Holy Spirit, teaching them to observe all things that I have commanded you; and lo, I am with you always, even to the end of the age."

Jeff was born in Dell Rapids, SD to a large family of two sisters and five brothers. He attended a private parochial school for all twelve years of his education. Coming from a family who loved music, he got involved in a rock band at an early age. They had high aspirations of some day making it big but their dreams were never fulfilled. Instead Jeff was introduced to the alcohol, drug and partying regimen so common to the rock band life style. Through it all, however, God's hand of protection was upon Jeff. One night he fell asleep in a drunken stupor inside his car with the thermometer registering frigid temperatures outside. He should have frozen to death but he survived the night. Another time Jeff fell asleep at the wheel while driving down the interstate. His car headed for the ditch but hit a guard rail and bounced off. It was becoming apparent that God had plans for him.

Jeff began to think often of the other side of life and wanted to know what it was like. He envisioned life as being in a movie and wanting to look beyond the screen. If he could only peek behind it and see what was on the other side! He nearly found out. He described to me a time when he was painting a picture of a man with an eagle's head. From behind his shoulder he could hear a voice asking, "Do you really want to see the other side of life?" When he acknowledged that he did, he had a vision of seeing himself in a casket. He knew that he would have to die in order to see what was beyond the curtain. At this moment another voice whispered to him, "Turn your head to the left if you want to see what is beyond this life." Jeff turned his head to the left but the other voice spoke to him in an urgent tone. "Turn your head to the right if you want to live." As the voices continued to speak, Jeff kept turning his head to the left. All the while he felt chains surround his ankles and then gradually creep up to his neck. He was about to turn his head to the left one last time when out of nowhere the palm of a hand slapped him across his forehead so hard that he fell backwards onto the floor. Jeff didn't know what had touched him but he noticed a change had come over himself. He wanted to find God. In his search he visited a monastery for a weekend but didn't find the answers he was looking for there.

After Jeff returned home, he moved in with an older brother, Steve, who was a Christian. Steve shared the gospel with Jeff and he accepted Jesus as his Savior. Shortly after that Steve invited him to go along with him to a prayer meeting at a small church he was attending. This was where Jeff had an encounter with the Holy Spirit that would forever change his life. He described it as fire coming out of every pore in his body. He knew then that it had been God Who had touched him three weeks earlier. Jeff saw every sin he had ever committed being purged from his body and burned up. This encounter set him up to becoming a missionary and pastor years later.

Jeff's first experience as a missionary was when he joined YWAM. He went to Belize where he attended a mission school. Later he boarded a schooner that was headed for Jamaica. A violent storm came up and the boat was tossed to and fro all day and all night. A beam cracked and the vessel began taking on water. An SOS was sent out and the British military answered the distress call by sending out a search aircraft. As the schooner was going down under the waves, the disheveled passengers managed to inflate and board a life raft. When each one was safely taken up in a helicopter and deposited back on land in Belize, Jeff discovered he had lost everything including his beloved guitar. When morning came and he heard the beautiful birds of Belize singing, he rejoiced and thanked God for His goodness in sparing his life once again.

Later on, Jeff would marry a lady named Ann who had been born and raised in Zimbabwe, Africa. She was of British descent. A lot of people had come over from England to settle there, a country which had previously been named Rhodesia. Because of his missionary heart, Jeff took Ann and moved there for a year to minister to the natives in the bush. Jeff knew that he had to find a way to reach these people in practical ways so he and his wife would glean the fields to collect the cabbages that had been left there to rot. They would put them in their truck and go to a high place on a hill and hand out the cabbages to the people. As they did, they invited them to come back for a Sunday service. This was the beginning of the "cabbage patch" churches that sprung up from a meager beginning of two and expand to over one hundred preaching points. These were areas in which people would meet under the trees to worship the Lord. Since Jeff and Ann returned to the United States the work they began has continued to grow and many buildings have been built to house the congregations.

Today Pastor Jeff is serving as the Senior Pastor/Missionary at the Hope Center of Lower Brule Indian Reservation in South Dakota. Prior to this call he served as a Children's and Senor Adult Pastor for 15 years. As Jeff has been faithful to serve God He has continued to open more doors to him. **Luke 16:10** - He who is faithful in what is least is faithful also in much.

Chapter 35

Jenna Haggar

Psalm 139:14–16 – I will praise You, for I am fearfully and wonderfully made; Marvelous are Your works, And that my soul knows very well. My frame was not hidden from You, When I was made in secret, And skillfully wrought in the lowest parts of the earth. Your eyes saw my substance, being yet unformed. And in Your book they all were written, The days fashioned for me, When as yet there were none of them.

Jenna was born in South Dakota's Capitol city, Pierre, SD. She was raised within a loving Christian family and was homeschooled along with her siblings. Her parents always emphasized the importance of serving others within the community and occasionally through political involvement. More than that, she was taught to follow Christ through education and by example.

After high school Jenna had an increasing desire to love and value others and the most intrinsic way she could do this was through what she considered to be the most fundamental right a person has - *life*. She became a pro life advocate when she was just 21 years old. She attributes much of her success in this area to a ministry, Summit, she attended in Colorado Springs where they emphasize Biblical leadership in all areas of life; political, business, education and many others. What you believe determines the direction of your life and ultimately, your destiny.

When she was 24 years old, Jenna was encouraged to seek political office. She was at first concerned because she didn't consider herself the "model politician." She didn't have any personal wealth; she didn't even have a college degree. But she was able to approach her campaign with a refreshing and unique perspective. It wasn't based on herself or her achievements but rather serving the people and truly representing their needs and desires. In a step of faith, she began knocking on doors and sharing a message with people letting them know she cared about them and the things that they were most concerned about. She won the respect of the people she met and was greatly encouraged by their support. Even though Jenna didn't necessarily expect to win, she trusted God and was rewarded with a tremendous victory.

As a State Senator, Jenna strives to represent people well and create for them a good government, where they can be proud to call themselves Americans. She has been supporting bills that protect the unborn and she also fights against the evils of human trafficking. She is the youngest elected female in South Dakota history

Jenna understands that since she has known Christ from the time she can remember, it would be very easy to fall into the trap of thinking she has no sin in her life. "Sometimes you have to fall to realize how much you are in need of Jesus Christ's authority over your life," she says. "The most important thing is a relationship with Christ and the biggest miracle besides salvation is realizing what one can't do and what He can do." She stressed the fact that one can be blinded to sin and yet God's grace goes to great depths to reach into a soul and awaken that person to it.

Sometimes people have a dream, a generational dream, where they place a false hope in the younger generations. They say it's the next generation that will take back America to its original roots of law and morality, but the truth is that regardless of gender, race or age we are the generation that's here and now. It's our responsibility to pursue righteousness and we all have the ability to make a difference and to live with a purpose to make all of our struggles worth it.

Jenna carefully seeks to follow God's plan for her life every day.

Chapter 36

Cashimaria Stroud

Jeremiah 29:11 - For I know the thoughts that I think toward you, says the Lord, thoughts of peace and not of evil, to give you a future and a hope.

Cashi was born in New York City and raised in Harlem along with seven brothers and sisters. Her father was very strict and stern, often beating his wife as well as Cashi. She suffered the horrors of being molested by an uncle. At the age of 16 she became pregnant and her father forced her boyfriend to marry her. This further added to Cashi's misery because her husband engaged in orgies with other women. Finally he released Cashi to get a divorce believing she couldn't live with him under those situations.

As a child, Cashi went to a parochial school where she learned to love Jesus even though she had no understanding of Him as Savior. That would come many years later. However the pain inside her grew to the point that she felt she had to relieve it through alcohol and drugs. After divorcing her husband, she married one more time. Neither of her spouses wanted to work so Cashi had to hold down a job to keep food on the table. Eventually this marriage also ended in a divorce.

At the age of 21, Cashi joined the Nation of Islam and became a Muslim. When the leader died, his son took over and introduced everyone to Islam from the East during which time Cashi learned to speak the Arabic language. Eventually she realized this wasn't the answer for her and she began to wander from religion to religion. She tried Buddhism, Jehovah's Witnesses, Christian Science, Mind Control, Transcendental Meditation, the School of Mystical Science, Scientology and just about everything else. However Cashi stopped short of experimenting with witchcraft. She sensed something very evil about it to the point of frightening her.

Things went from bad to worse for Cashi and she lost custody of her son because she was practicing Buddhism and was on welfare. This threw her into a deep depression and she finally wound up having a nervous breakdown. While in a mental hospital she was heavily dosed with drugs. As soon as she was released she quit taking them and went back to crack cocaine. From March 1985 to May 1987, Cashi was homeless and was shuffled around in shelters which were especially equipped for the mentally ill. Afterward she went to a welfare hotel where she lived for eight years in a virtual hell of being raped, molested and sodomized on an almost daily basis. It was here where she tried to commit suicide by overdosing on pills.

One day, a little sunshine crept into Cashi's life when a French man came to her door and gave her a Bible. He urged her to read **Jeremiah 29:11** which became her salvation verse. Cashi went to live at Walter Hoven Home for six months where she was immersed in the Bible and prayer. After that she went back to the hotel where she once more returned to drugs. Shortly after that she was asked to leave due to her mental state which caused her to have fits of violence. Before she left, a counselor led Cashi in a prayer to receive Jesus as her personal Savior. This happened in September 28, 1995. The counselor recommended a 15 month Christian program where Cashi once again was steeped in the Bible. She even joined a choir where she loved to sing. She stayed clean from drugs and alcohol for five years so her mother allowed her to move south to live with her. It wasn't long after that when Cashi fell back and began using crack cocaine again. Each time she got high, she cried out to God for help. Cashi believed God had forsaken her but she never lost her trust in Jesus Christ. By the time she moved to Sioux Falls she had given up drugs but still went on drinking binges. Meanwhile she felt the Holy Spirit groaning within her because of the deep hurts. Finally she called the Help Line. They directed her to go to an AA meeting. She went and met a man who told her that his "higher power" was Jesus Christ. Cashi also received counseling from a local priest for three months who taught her about the Father's love. She believes that God led her to AA because it was here where she got her faith and trust back. All desire for drugs, alcohol and even cigarettes left her and she became a completely new person. Her anger towards Father God disappeared and was replaced by a consuming love just like she had always had for His Son Jesus.

Today Cashi is involved with Al Anon and the Children of Alcoholics. She is the sponsor of ten people who have been addicted to alcohol and gambling. She told me that the only way she can stay in God's grace is to share her life in Christ with others along with the Word of God. She is so immersed in Christ that He is her entire reason for existence. Cashi is single today and has no desire to marry again unless God brings along a man who is completely sold out to Jesus.

Cashi told me that God will lead people in different ways and has many ways of setting them free. She often reflects on **John 8:36** which states, "So if the Son makes you free, you will be free indeed."

Chapter 37

Russell Willingham

John 14:6 – Jesus said to him, "I am the way, the truth, and the life. No one comes to the Father except through Me."

Russell was born in San Jose, CA on December 14, 1961. He spent a good share of his life in Southern California where his father was a roofer and his mother a homemaker. He had a younger brother named Kenny. This was during the time of the sexual revolution and hippy movement. Russell had vague memories of seeing nightly newscasts of the Viet Nam War as a young child.

When Russell was seven years old, his mother had a baby girl who died of S.I.D.S. at the age of three months. This threw his mother into an emotional tail spin. Russell starkly remembers seeing a fireman carry the dead body of his sister while his mother followed, wailing loudly. This tragedy resulted in the end of an already poor marriage for his parents.

Russell described his childhood as a particularly stormy period in his life. His emotionally unstable mother would fly into rages often causing him and his brother to cower inside. While Russell would escape through a world of fantasy, Kenny would lie face down on his bed and bounce up and down for comfort. His mother believed God had rained down judgment on her by taking her beloved daughter from her. While she was outward in her expressions, Russell's father was inward and unexpressive which caused even more anger and resentment.

Up to this point his mother never drank but his father was a heavy drinker. But when his mother moved to Texas with the two boys to live with their grandparents, she took a job as a cocktail waitress in a bar and her drinking began. By this time the family had moved out of the grandparent's house and rented an apartment. When Russell's mother couldn't find a babysitter for the boys, she took them with her and parked them in a back room of the bar while she worked. Russell and his brother felt deep despair and abandonment.

As Russell thought back on his childhood he remembered being quite artistic. He loved to draw pictures. He also felt bonded with his dad but never his mother. Even though his dad had a drinking problem he wanted his boys to know God so he would take them to church and read Bible stories to them at night. He would discipline them but in a way that caused Russell to respect him and not fear him like he did his mother.

Russell remembers walking home and seeing a magazine lying in the grass. He was around seven or eight years old at the time. He picked it up and began looking at the pictures of the nude women within. This opened something up inside him. He felt nurtured in a weird way that filled a deep psychological need and he was instantaneously addicted to pornography. "I felt more of a bonding with the women in the magazine than my own mother," Russell remarked.

From that time on he would look at porn regularly because it was a world of pleasure and escape. This was the beginning of his sexual addiction that would keep him in bondage for years. He loved reading the Ian Fleming novels (James Bond), anything fantasy/sci-fi, and anything having to do with the occult. He would watch hours of horror movies, not realizing that he was welcoming demonic things into his soul.

At age twelve, a positive change came into Russell's life. He and two of his friends went to a Christian movie. After the movie they went forward in response to a message about God's forgiveness to receive Jesus as their Savior. He remembered feeling so clean inside and the first thing he wanted to do was to stop cursing (that was the biggest "sin" in his life that he was aware of at the time). Yet because of his torrid home life, he quickly drifted away from God and continued in his destructive habits.

As a sixteen-year-old, Russell decided he no longer wanted to live with the alcoholism and revolving boyfriends of his mother. So he wrote a letter to his dad. Russell didn't know where he lived so he sent it to his grandmother who passed it along. Russell stated in the letter that he wanted to live with him so when his father received it; he drove hundreds of miles to pick him up and move Russell back with him to Southern California.

Although his dad still drank and used drugs, he was spiritually hungry and he and Russell would often talk late into the night about the things of God. Russell picked up a Bible and began reading it for himself for the first time in his life. Though the porn and some occult practices were still going on Scripture began having an effect. God used this to prepare him for a sincere return to His Son Jesus Christ. He soon found himself traveling to the East coast with a lady he barely knew. On the way, they stopped in Ohio where they met up with a very "on fire" woman of God named Hazel.

Hazel straightened out Russell's thinking by explaining to him that the New Age philosophy and practices he was dabbling in were satanic. The next morning (a Saturday), Russell climbed a three story school building where he began pouring his heart out to God. He continued to fast and pray and determine in his heart he was going to follow the Lord all his life. He wanted only the truth and no more lies.

This was the beginning of his deliverance from sexual addiction. By the time he reached Boston, he had read some good Christian books about basic biblical truth, theology and apologetics. Upon returning to Yucca Valley, he found a good church where he sat under the teaching and preaching of a good solid pastor who built a strong foundation under Russell. This was when Russell met Keri who he married and had a son and daughter together.

Russell became a youth pastor and worked in evangelism as well. He went to Fresno and planted a little church. Later he became an associate pastor in another small church. Nevertheless, Russell would struggle with periods when he would feel abandoned inside. This would cause him to make demands on his wife she wasn't able to fulfill which, in turn, created a strain on the marriage. Russell knew something was wrong so he went to a Christian therapist. At first he believed the problem lay primarily with his wife but as he proceeded in the therapy he learned that the dilemma lay mostly at his doorstep.

Russell explained to me that his behavior was rooted in the fact that his unmet need for maternal love caused him to demand it from his wife. He finally understood that his wife couldn't give him that but Jesus was the only one who could. God spoke to his heart one day, "Russell, you are trying to fill a need through your wife that only I can satisfy. You are making her into an idol." He was convicted of this and realized he was looking to her for approval instead of Jesus.

God led Russell to New Creation Ministries – a ministry that helps people get set free from their sexual addictions. He volunteered for a year and a half and then left a lucrative job to join the staff full time. Surprisingly most of the people who came to MCM were Christians who had been caught up in porn. "7 out of 10 Christian men look at it," Russell told me. He also went on to tell me that some pastors are in denial that members of their congregation struggle with this very thing. "It is obvious that we are sexually broken in our culture," Russell stated. He was so concerned about the commonality of Christian men being caught up in pornography that he wrote a book called "Breaking Free" in 1999 to instruct men about how to become free from sexual addiction.

In the small groups at New Creation Ministries, people are encouraged to be very honest with one another about their addictions. The leaders are also transparent about their struggles even though they have found much deliverance by the Spirit of God. This opens up a door for the others to boldly step forward to acknowledge where they are in their lives. According to **James 5:16**, this is a very healthy thing to do and has resulted in many experiencing deep inner healing.

In 2013 his wife of thirty years passed away from cancer. A year later, Russell met and married Paula. "Jesus has poured his bountiful, extravagant love on me. THIS is what eventually broke the back of sexual addiction in my life," Russell told me.

James 5:16 – Confess your sins to one another, and pray for one another, that you may be healed. The effective, fervent prayer of a righteous man avails much.

Chapter 38

Jim Bolin

Genesis 12:1 – Now the Lord said to Abram, "Go forth from your country, and from your relatives and from your father's house, to the land which I will show you.

Jim was born on December 31, 1950 in Portland, Oregon. He was raised in what he described to me as a wonderful Christian family along with a sister and two brothers. He put his faith in Jesus at a very young age.

After Jim graduated from college in which he majored in history, he decided to see some of the world and so he volunteered to teach in a mission school in Africa in the small nation of Swaziland. He taught at the Mankayane High School, a boarding school for Swazi students, for three years during the 1970's.It was in Africa that Jim met a fellow teacher named Ruth Mielke. They became engaged in 1978 and in 1979 were married in the United States. Both Jim and Ruth were interested in boarding school education at that time. Returning to the United States, they soon heard of a small boarding school in central South Dakota, the Sunshine Bible Academy. Jim and Ruth moved to South Dakota in 1981 and began a four year stint as a teacher and coach at the school. Boarding schools require great commitment in that it is more of a lifestyle than a job with constant interaction between students and staff. Both Jim and Ruth enjoyed the Sunshine experience and even today keep in contact with students and staff from the past.

During their time in rural South Dakota, the Bolins began the process of adoption. In both 1984 and later in 1988 they adopted two baby boys and over the next twenty years raised them to maturity. Both boys are now married and the Bolins now have one grandchild. In the mid 1980's the Bolins left Sunshine so that Jim could work on an advanced degree from the University of South Dakota. When that was accomplished they moved to Canton where they have lived since 1987. From 1987 until

2010, Jim taught in the public schools concentrating on the teaching of American history. Jim also was involved in coaching a variety of sports and served as athletic director of the school system for eleven years.

In 2007 Jim decided to run for a political office in Canton. The city was embroiled in a scandal that involved the misuse of city funds and many folks were very upset with city government. Jim ran for a city council position and won by a large margin. Later he became the mayor of the town as it transitioned to a new form of city government.

In 2008 Jim was elected to the state legislature where he continues to serve in the House of Representatives. He represents the small towns of Alcester, Beresford, Canton and Elk Point in the legislature. He has been voted in by the people four times and has enjoyed his service for the state, despite the long drive to Pierre each weekend during the winter. Jim has worked to promote traditional values in Pierre and enjoys the give and take of the political process. Jim says, "You will not win every battle in the political arena. You will take some knocks and you will get bruised, figuratively speaking, by some of the events that take place in the capitol city. However, it is a pleasure to serve the people and to defend what you think is right."

Besides his faith and family which has always been first for Jim, campaigning comes next on his list of enjoyable things to do. Many people who hold public office do not enjoy campaigning but Jim enjoys people and likes interacting with them. Jim sees the holding of public office as a way to help the public understand the government better and to provide necessary services for our state. Jim also enjoys competitive sports and visiting historical sites.

Jim is most thankful for his salvation, his wife and his good health. He has hardly had a sick day in his life and feels most fortunate for that great blessing. He believes that a healthy life style of abstinence from tobacco and alcohol has been a benefit in his life.

When I asked Jim what brought him to South Dakota, he said it was "the hand of God" because there was no other reason for him and his wife to settle down here. God certainly has a purpose for them to be here because He needs people like Jim Bolin serving Him in Pierre. Jim has been a positive biblical influence for the culture as he has supported many pro-family bills during his time in the legislature. He doesn't know yet what the future contains for him but he isn't ruling out a possible run for the State Senate in 2016. Only time will tell.

Chapter 39

Vivian (Shillander) Ellis

2 Corinthians 11:13-14 – For such are false apostles, deceitful workers, transforming themselves into apostles of Christ. And no wonder! For Satan himself transforms himself into an angel of light.

Vivian was born in Anamosa, IA after WW II when her father was studying to become a minister. She was the youngest of four children. Her mother had had a stark conversion experience after her first husband died. It was after that when she met Vivian's father at Dakota Wesleyan University. After he graduated he was assigned to churches in small towns all over South Dakota. As a child in Sunday school, Vivian first gave her heart to Jesus. She remembers singing the song, "Come into my heart, Lord Jesus." It was when she started second grade in the fall that she realized something had changed within her. She no longer joined the other children who teased the boy with learning disabilities. Instead she felt compassion toward him and she remembers thinking, "What happened to me?" Vivian's childhood was a happy wonderful time in her life. In 1968 her mother passed away when she was only 15 years old. Her father remarried a year later and moved to his home town of Miller. She was the only one of the children still at home. Vivian remembers how her father would work with her stepmother to try to have a more positive attitude towards life instead of being such a "worry wart." A year later, Vivian left to go to Dakota Wesleyan University.

During this period of Vivian's life, she was feeling quite distraught and lost. She even experienced a day when she was questioning whether there was even a God or not. When she looked up out the dorm window and saw the tops of the evergreen trees, she realized there has to be a Creator. They were just too perfect and too beautiful! She prayed and asked God to give her something worthwhile to do with her life.

That summer Vivian hitchhiked to San Francisco with a couple of other girls. In Golden Gate Park while attending a "hippie" event, they encountered a couple of young men carrying a guitar and saying something to everyone they passed. As they passed them, they said, "Hey! Do you know Jesus?" Vivian said, "Yes, I know Jesus." Her friends said, "Oh, Jesus Freaks!" In short time her friends dismissed themselves and said they would come back and get her later. Quite a bit of time passed, so Vivian ended up going with the young men to the group head quarters on the beach. They called themselves the Children of God whose leader, a self proclaimed prophet, was David Berg. At the time, Vivian didn't realize she was about to become part of a cult. She thought they were solid believers because they sounded so "Christian." They memorized two scripture verses a day and read five chapters from the Bible in their private time, and then came together as a group to study the Bible for an additional four hours each day. They lived communally and shared everything exactly as the early church had done in **Acts 4:32-34** – "Now the multitude of those who believed were of one heart and one soul; neither did anyone say that any of the things he possessed was his own, but they had all things in common. And with great power the apostles gave witness to the resurrection of the Lord Jesus. And great grace was upon them all. Nor was there anyone among them who lacked; for all who were possessors of lands or houses sold them and brought the proceeds of the things that were sold." It all sounded so right and good to Vivian so two days later she joined the group. She thought it was the best Christian organization in the world.

One of the first things Vivian learned was how to witness to others and share the gospel. Along with the others, she had to give up all her personal possessions and agenda to reach the world for Christ. Vivian told me there was no "hanky pank" allowed in the group when she joined. She felt there was nothing wrong with all this because everything they did was accompanied with a Bible verse. They were all young people who were excited to share the Word of God with others.

Before Vivian knew what was happening, she found herself gradually being sucked into the deception that hovered over the group. The leader told her as well as the others that she had to cut off all relations with her family lest she be "tempted to go back to Egypt." Eventually she met a man within the group whom she married. Together they had five children. The "Children of God" were constantly being taught about the end times and, according to David Berg, there was an impending nuclear disaster coming. Vivian and her husband's job in the group were to manage a refuge farm near Spokane, Washington. When the disaster didn't come as the leader had prophesied, they sold everything and moved to Europe. They landed in Spain with their three children and another one on the way. They had only $800 to their name and nowhere to go and no idea of where any more money would come from. But God graciously took care of them. They found a summer home to rent in a village south of Barcelona. Vivian's husband spoke at an Anglican Church and met a woman from the village who took them under her wing and paid their rent. Eventually they were able to bring in finances by playing the guitar and singing. After their performances in restaurants they passed a plate for donations. This was a common practice all over Europe, Vivian told me.

After three years, Vivian and her husband left their four children with another couple from the "Children of God" group and went to Paris for a month where they earned $4000 by performing in the Metro (subway station) and also in restaurants. From there they went to Holland where they bought a van which they converted into a camper. For the next three years they lived in it while they traveled all over Spain, France, and Belgium singing. This form of income was sanctioned by the group, because, as one was performing, they were witnessing to people about the love of Jesus. Their youngest son was born in Belgium in 1983. When the baby was six months old, the couple moved to Thailand. The policy of the group was to go into the entire world and preach the gospel to every creature. Vivian felt like she was going to finally be the missionary she had always wanted to be in a third world country. Yet by this time the gospel had been severely tainted by David Berg.

While in Thailand, Vivian was disappointed to learn the members of the group were not behaving as missionaries should. They lived with a family who wasn't very nice to the little Thai maid. Vivian began to realize that things were terribly wrong and at a meeting she began to voice her opinion about it. The other people there immediately stopped the meeting and went into a corner to talk about Vivian. One of them came and took the baby out of her arms. Vivian thought for a moment they might actually throw her out that night - out onto the street. Eventually they all went to bed and Vivian went up to her bedroom as well. When her husband informed her that she was really in trouble, she decided she should write a letter of repentance and quietly slide it under the door of the head couple of the house. The next morning nothing had changed. She was shunned by all in the house. She realized her only friend was the young Thai maid.

This was to be the beginning of a nightmare that would last for several years. After three days, the "District Shepherd" told Vivian to "get rid of the devil that she was listening to." Her only response was what Martin Luther had said to the council at the Diet of Worms, "Here I stand by the grace of God. I can do no other." This sealed her fate that she was "a lost cause" so her things were gathered and she was put in a car while they figured out where to take her. They found the cheapest hotel around which had been built during the Viet Nam War to be used as an R and R for the American soldiers. Vivian found herself in a room no larger than a prison cell. She was told not to come back to the house or to try to see her children. Her husband was to bring the baby to her twice a day for her to nurse him. But on the third day, he brought the baby along with all his things, saying that they decided Vivian would be happier if she had at least one of the children. They couldn't find another mother for him anyway.

For two months Vivian subsisted on two scanty meals of Cow Pot which consisted of nothing but rice, vegetables and egg along with a slice of cucumber. Then her sister made arrangements to fly Vivian and the baby back to the U.S. in July of 1984.

Sometime around 1986, Vivian had gotten the name of a Christian lawyer. He began to help her work on how she could get the other children back. (He was kind enough to donate all his time free of charge.) Also around that time, she had gone to Senator Pressler's office to ask how our government might be able to help. In May of 1987, Vivian's father passed away, leaving her a small inheritance. In June of that year, Vivian appealed to the Billy Graham organization for help. They connected her with a church in Sioux Falls where Vivian met other families who also had lost children to a cult. This one was called End Time Ministries/Overcomers and it also focused on the end times with the people striving to live like the early church totally separated from the world. She had also heard of private investigators out of Missouri who had helped rescue children from the same cult who were living in South America. In December of 1987 Vivian left for Thailand to try to locate her children. Before leaving she had a dream that her children would be handed over to her with no problem. However, when she reached Thailand, she found herself in a grueling search for nearly two months. She employed one of the private investigators to come and help her look for her children. They learned that her husband had to renew his visa at the immigration office in Bangkok. They made arrangements with the Thai official to have her husband take him to where the children were. The investigators followed. They also had gotten the media involved and ABC's 20/20 planned to film the event in case the cult would try to take the children and hide them in another country. By this time the group was in around 100 different nations. The immigration officer, along with the investigators made her husband bring the children to Vivian. She handed him the legal papers which gave her temporary custody of the children. Then Vivian left with her unwilling children to catch a plane back to the U.S. At this time they ranged in ages from 8 to 13 years old. They resented Vivian and refused to cooperate with her in any way. She got discouraged even though many people tried to help her.

27 years later, Vivian regrets that she didn't trust the Lord enough with her problem, thinking it was too great to apply the Bible to. However she knows the Lord has been working in her situation as difficult as it has been. Her ex-husband went back to the Mormon religion and got her daughter involved in it. Vivian's middle son was a victim of suicide and another son has turned his back on her. Her youngest son teaches at a community college. Her oldest returned to Thailand to live and has Vivian's youngest granddaughter there. Vivian has one grandson and eight granddaughters today. She is praying for them all, believing that one day they will all decide to follow Jesus!

"The best thing that has happened to me most recently is Bible Study Fellowship, International," Vivian told me. She has recommitted her life to "not doubt God, to study to show herself approved, and to run the race with patience."

Several years ago, Vivian prayed and asked God to give her a new husband as she had been single for 13 years. She specifically told God what she wanted in a mate – someone who was kind, gentle, and loving like her father had been and someone who was tall and of normal weight. She ended her prayer by telling the Lord that she didn't even care if he was handicapped. God heard and answered that prayer. Vivian met this man who was residing in assisted living in 1996 and, at 19 years of age, had suffered a Traumatic Brain Injury. Later they were married and Vivian believes God will heal him. They have made plans to visit a brain center in Texas.

Vivian shares her story with the hope she can help someone else avoid the same mistakes she has made. Her desire is for people to find the one true God through Jesus Christ, our Savior and to avoid the false gods, prophets, and apostles of this present world.

Amen!!! (Vivian's footnote)

Chapter 40

John Glasser

Romans 10:15 – And how shall they preach unless they are sent? As it is written: "How beautiful are the feet of those who preach the gospel of peace, Who bring glad tidings of good things!"

John was born in Wildwood, GA. His father was a pastor and the family moved from there to California. After several more moves in that state, they finally wound up in Wyoming where they spent several years. When John was in high school he began drifting away from God. He had no desire to go to a Christian college but he finally agreed to go to the University of Sioux Falls. It was on a football field when John came face to face with the Lord and gave his life to Jesus Christ. Because he saw how his family struggled financially, he didn't want to go into the ministry. He didn't think he could properly support a family that way so he got a business degree instead. He began his first job at Gateway. After three years, Gateway was on its way out so John began a new job at Verizon where he became manager. All this time God had been tugging at his heart to serve Him in ministry but John resisted. Finally he relented and began working for the University of Sioux Falls as a fund raiser. It was here that Reed DeVries approached John about getting involved with First Priority.

John accepted God's calling to join First Priority and his first job there was fund raising. He fell in love with the students and the desire to see them excel drove John to become involved more deeply. It wasn't long until he had the opportunity to meet the founder of the organization – Benny Proffitt. After John listened to Benny's vision, he was eager to travel with him around the nation to share it with the churches. The vision had to do with preparing students to share the gospel amongst their peers.

After John returned to Sioux Falls, he met a girl, Bethany, who shared her heart's desire to see the students at her school get on fire for Christ.

John helped her start a group at her school where a student team would gather together to hold an assembly. During this time they would sing and worship and encourage other students to dream big and let them know they have a story to share.

Today John serves as City Director of First Priority in Sioux Falls. First Priority focuses on the middle and high school students. Their mission is to unite, empower, and serve. Their vision is to unite and empower the church to bring the hope of Jesus Christ to every student. They have groups located all across the nation.

Chapter 41

Sue Mutziger

Psalm 30:2-3 - O Lord my God, I pleaded to you and you gave me my health again. You brought me back from the brink of the grave, from death itself, and now I am alive!

Sue was born in Mitchell, SD in 1950. She grew up on a farm south of Mitchell near the little town of Ethan. She was born into a loving family, having two sisters and one brother. She enjoyed the simple, humble life of growing up on a farm.

Although Sue's family attended a church every Sunday where she learned "about" God, she says she didn't experience having a personal relationship with Jesus. "I don't remember this ever being explained to me," says Sue. As a little girl, however, she says she remembers hungering to know God. She would pump her swing as high as it would go hoping to reach the tree tops where she believed God was. There she hoped to find Him.

"In those days it was frowned upon to be involved in or attend evangelical services," states Sue. She remembers catching the Oral Roberts TV show every once in a while and how she would hunger to listen to it in its entirety. Looking back on her life as a youngster Sue states she realizes now that she knew something was missing from her life but she didn't know what it was.

Sue went to a country grade school and then attended Ethan High School until her graduation. She had a strong desire to go to college but back then young ladies were expected to either become a nurse or a teacher or marry their high school sweetheart. Sue had no deep desire to do any of those things but decided she would try nursing. After she started her higher education she switched her major to social work.

Sue's desire to know God became a reality during her junior year at college. She went to see the popular musical "Jesus Christ Superstar" when it came to the campus. This caused her to question who Jesus was. The lyrics were, "Jesus Christ, Superstar, are you who you say you are?" She prayed, "God I need to know you. Please become real to me; reveal yourself to me." This caused Sue to continue her search with even more diligence and purpose.

Sue was not aware of it at the time but the Lord had laid it on the heart of one of her college classmates to pray for her. Sue recalls one night in February, 1971 returning to her dormitory room after attending an evening class. She says a voice spoke to her and said, "Sue, you have sin in your life and you need to repent."

As she entered her dormitory room the power of the Holy Spirit fell upon her and she found herself weeping sorrowfully over her sins. (In a flash the Lord took her back to the age of 6 years of age to the present pointing out to her the things she needed to repent of.) Sue states she felt the joy of an inner cleansing. As she sat on her bed gazing out the window she saw what she described as a bright golden light that shone across the sky. When she approached the window to take a closer look a vision of Jesus appeared to her. "He was radiant and looking right into my eyes," states Sue. His arms outstretched He said, "Behold! Come unto me, my child!"

Realizing a new found joy and peace that she had never experienced before and wanting to share that with someone, the only person she could think of was Alice...the person who had been praying for her. Sue took off running across campus to find Alice. When she entered Alice's room Alice stated, "Sue your face is aglow! I know what has happened to you... you found Jesus tonight didn't you? You got born again!"

Alice then shared the gospel with Sue explaining the salvation message. She also shared what it means to be born again and explained the

Baptism of the Holy Spirit. This is the first time Sue had ever heard about having a personal relationship with Jesus Christ; it was the first time she had ever heard of the Baptism of the Holy Spirit. Alice then invited Sue to begin attending the Bible studies and prayer meetings that were being held on campus.

After Sue graduated from college she moved to Minneapolis and opened up an office center. She states that she has always had excellent office skills and enjoyed this kind of work. It was here where she met her future husband. They married and had a daughter together but the marriage did not last long.

When Sue's daughter was five years old Sue entered graduate school; she earned a Masters Degree in Family Counseling. For the next 15 years Sue enjoyed her career in the cities. She felt on top of the world having completed a higher education degree and enjoying a career that comfortably supported herself and her daughter.

Sue's parents were now living in Mitchell (2007) where her father began to experience health issues. In an attempt to keep her father from having to be placed in a nursing home, Sue made the decision to return to Mitchell to assist her mother in the care of her father. By making this move Sue's career was greatly impacted: she was no longer able to be employed in her profession without updating her credentials or going back to school. At this point in her life Sue decided this just didn't make good financial sense. Because Sue had other skills to fall back on she took other kinds of employment.

In April 2012 Sue was diagnosed with colon cancer. Her doctor recommended chemotherapy but Sue decided to try some holistic treatment instead and to put her trust in the Lord to heal her. The doctor told her that there was always the possibility that the cancer could reappear in another part of her body.

Sue was working two jobs so her prayer life, it seemed, was always put on the back burner. She knew this was not good but didn't know how to fix it.

Eighteen months later the cancer resurfaced: she now had a small nodule, one on each lung. She decided that it was now time to get serious about her walk with the Lord. She fully realized that her faith was not where it should be if she ever needed to call upon Jesus to heal her of cancer. Although she had never been an avid TV watcher she decided that the few hours per week that she was spending on it could be better spent with the Lord. She decided to have the cable to her TV disconnected.

It was at this time that a woman from her Bible study gave Sue a small booklet entitled "Healed of Cancer" by Dodie Osteen. (She is the mother of Pastor Joel Osteen, a well known evangelist from Houston, Texas.) In the book Dodie describes how she was healed from terminal cancer by learning how to stand on God's Biblical promises. Dodie began to memorize Scripture verses on healing and she recited them every day until she began to feel better. Now it is 34 years later and Dodie (who is 89 years of age) is alive and well and serving the Lord in full time ministry. Jesus healed her of cancer.

Sue wavered in her thoughts: would God heal her? After reading the book many times over she finally decided that God could heal her, too. Sue began to memorize the healing Scripture verses. Wherever she went she took that little book with her. One verse that particularly stood out to her was **Jeremiah 30:17** -For I will restore health to you, says the Lord, and I will heal you of your wounds!

March of 2015 brought unfortunate news. A cough and labored breathing developed. Sue went to the emergency room where it was discovered that the cancer had spread extensively in her lungs. She now had stage 4 lung cancer. She went home to get her legal affairs in order.

The Bible says to be prudent and wise but Sue always continued to trust that Jesus was going to heal her.

Sue's health deteriorated rapidly. Her lungs were closing in on her; she felt like there was 25 pounds of bricks pressing in on her chest. Within a couple of days she was back in the emergency room. After a two day stay in the hospital the doctor informed her there was nothing else that the medical profession could do for her.

The doctor sent her home with a hand- held nebulizer. This only afforded her temporary relief. The doctor told her that instead of returning to the hospital she needed to enter hospice. Sue realized that unless Jesus stepped in and performed a miracle she only had a couple of days left to live. Her breathing had become excruciatingly labored and she was forced to use the nebulizer every 5 - 10 minutes. By now Sue was not able to sleep in her bed; she was only able to rest in her recliner.

At 10:00 PM Sue slipped into the recliner knowing that this was going to be a very long night. Now her goal was just to get through the night. By 11:30 PM panic began to set in. It was as though someone had forced a pillowcase over her head. "Not being able to breathe is a scary thing," states Sue. I knew the feeling as I had experienced this myself in the past – not being able to breathe when I was suddenly and gravely taken ill in Peru, South America. But that's a story for another time.

Sue realized that she needed to remain calm; otherwise her situation would become so much worse. She began reciting the scripture verses she had learned over the past 18 months. She discovered that when she kept her mind on the Bible verses she was able to remain calm; when she let her mind drift panic would once more set in.

By 1:30 in the morning, Sue realized that she could not go on. She cried out to the Lord, "I need you now, Jesus... not two hours from now, not one hour from now, not five minutes from now. I need you right now because I can't breathe."

An unfriendly frightening voice spoke into her left ear saying, "Do you still trust Jesus with your health?" Sue soon realized it was the enemy speaking to her. Because of her close walk with Jesus she could answer him assuredly saying, "Yes, yes, I trust Jesus with my health!"

Then a voice she recognized whispered into her right ear saying, **John 10:10** - "The thief comes to steal, to kill, and to destroy, but I have come that you might have life and that you might have it more abundant!" Sue knew that illness doesn't come from the Lord but from the enemy but it was as though she was being asked to say it out loud.

As soon as she declared this with her mouth saying, "Lord, I don't believe for one minute that you gave me this disease… I know it is from the enemy" the seemingly pile of bricks lifted from her chest; her lungs instantly opened up and she began to breathe normally. She wondered "how many of these breaths am I going to get?" She began to count and when she got up to six she fell asleep. When she awakened, it was 7 AM. She recalls opening her eyes and looking up at the white ceiling. She was amazed to realize that she didn't die during the night but was still alive!

Sue's health is excellent today and she is active in ministry. **Psalm 118:17** says, " I shall not die but live and proclaim the works of the Lord." Sue says it is important that she share with others what the Lord has done for her. "Healing is for everyone," states Sue. Like Dodie, Sue believes it was the power of the Word of God that healed her. She would like to encourage those who read her testimony to read the Word of God, to build their faith and then to never stop believing for their miracle!

Chapter 42

Pastor Kenneth Hunt

Samuel 15:22b – Behold, to obey is better than sacrifice, And to heed than the fat of rams.

In 1955, Ken was born at Good Fellow Air Force Base in San Angelo, TX to Dave and Bo Hunt. He is the youngest of four sons and has a younger sister.

When Ken was 7 years old, he gave his heart to Christ but it wasn't until he was 13 that he understood how much God loved him. Because of this knowledge, Ken sought to serve him but it was in his own strength. He soon became crushed under the burden of trying to serve the Lord this way. This caused him to waver back and forth in his faith.

When Ken was 28, he had a breakthrough when he finally understood that his job was simply to obey and leave the results up to God. This was when he felt a calling into the ministry. He and his wife prayed about where to go to school and God led them to Sioux Falls, SD to check out the seminary there. Ken felt God wanted him there but his wife was afraid and had doubts so they returned to Washington State where their home church was.

They sought God for a clear sign of direction and after four months of prayer, Ken came home from work one day to find his wife in tears. She had been reading the Bible and came under conviction that she had allowed fear to keep her from trusting God. She agreed with Ken that it was God's will for him to go to the seminary in Sioux Falls. It wasn't ten minutes later when the phone rang. It was a man from the seminary on the other end of the line offering Ken a scholarship. Also his wife was given a provisional scholarship to the school.

Because of their obedience, God moved ahead of Ken and his wife to prepare the way for them. Within a day they found a house and God opened doors before them and blessed them amazingly.

After seminary, Ken took many interim positions to help square away problems in several churches. When he took a pastoral position in Huron, the church had been losing many members and most of the people remaining were 70 years old or older. The situation seemed hopeless but they prayed for a year. Then there was a breakthrough. Some people from Burma started to attend. They were Karens. Before long more Karens began to come and soon there were 350 in attendance. Ken had to start a second service in the church. By the time Ken had left the church there were 600 Karens coming. Ken had learned that when he was obedient God worked.

Ken shared with me some miracles in his life. One time God protected him and his family from carbon monoxide poisoning. Another time his dog was run over but was uninjured. One day his daughter fell 15 feet towards a concrete slab at his house but instead of hitting the hard surface, God had somehow caused her to fall onto a soft grassy spot and she wasn't hurt.

God blessed Ken in many ways. Whenever he prayed and sought God for help in his ministry, He would send people to come alongside. When he was serving in a church in Washington State, he partnered with the Union Gospel Mission there and 18 men were baptized.

For the last several years God has been using Ken in prison ministry. He is now a full time pastor to the women's prison in Pierre, SD. Ken shared with me how God has done such an amazing work among the prisoners there. 90 women have been baptized during the two years that he has been working full time with them. Of these women many are helping in the ministry to counsel and lead others to Jesus as their Savior and Lord.

Ken and his wife just seek to obey and every time they do, they see God move in mighty ways.

Chapter 43

Glenna Remington

Matthew 6:33 – But seek first His kingdom and His righteousness, and all these things will be added to you.

Glenna was born in Huron, SD but grew up in the little town of Conde near Aberdeen, SD. She had seven brothers and a little sister who arrived on the scene when Glenna was 11 years old. Although she and her family were active church goers, she never had a personal relationship with Jesus until later on in life.

Trouble began for Glenna when she was seven years old and was sexually molested. This caused a lot of depression and a low self image which followed her for many years to come.

After Glenna started college at SDSU in Brookings, she was introduced to the reality of Jesus Christ. She went to see the movie "The Cross and The Switchblade" where she made a decision to invite Jesus into her heart. She also attended a couple of prayer meetings on campus but didn't continue. Instead she put God on a back burner and focused on getting her teaching degree. After transferring to Northern State University she graduated.

Glenna taught in one school close to home before winding up in Sioux Falls to teach at a Catholic elementary school. It was here when Glenna began to date a man who pressured her into having a sexual relationship with him. When she discovered that she was pregnant her boyfriend insisted she get an abortion. She refused and the man disappeared from her life. She never saw him again.

Glenna resigned from her teaching job and got involved in selling cookware and had an opportunity to go to Rapid City to promote it there. A kind representative offered to let her stay in the basement of her house. During this time in her life, Glenna needed someone to encourage her and she soon met that person at a laundromat. The lady had a countenance that was full of joy. She invited her to come to her house to show the cookware at her home. When Glenna arrived there was the lady's Christian family there who had been studying the Bible during their dinner time. They reached out to Glenna and showed her a lot of love and support. They prayed with her to rededicate her life to Christ and invited her to visit their charismatic church in Rapid City. Glenna was amazed that nobody judged her for being an unwed mother. Instead they poured God's love and acceptance upon her. They even held a baby shower for her. This left an indelible impression on Glenna.

In July of 1977 a son was born to Glenna and she named him Ryan. Two months later she met Larry whom she would marry. During this time in her life, Glenna had been baptized and filled with the Holy Spirit. Glenna knew that God had a special plan in bringing them together because Larry had an inner urging to come to Rapid City from the state of Washington around the same time Glenna moved there, and attend the church where they met. After Larry and Glenna were married Larry adopted Ryan as his own son. They were also blessed to have another son, Philip and a daughter, Hannah.

In 1991, the couple moved back to Eastern South Dakota where they helped start a church in Groton. God opened up many doors there for Glenna. In the years to come she became the area board president for Aglow International for Eastern South Dakota. She also got involved as a paraprofessional in the RTI program at the elementary school in Groton where she taught reading and math.

At the church they attended, Glenna and her husband served on the worship team. Also Glenna was a Deaconess and in charge of setting up a monthly day of 24 hours of prayer, praying for our government's leaders.

When Glenna was 50 years old, God urged her to write a letter to the man who had molested her as a child. In the letter, she told him that she forgave him. Years later, Glenna met the man outside a store and he asked her to forgive him for what he had done. She had the opportunity right then and there to lead him to Christ.

Glenna is thankful to the women in Aglow who helped her find inner healing from the wounds she had suffered because of her experience as a child. She is also very thankful that she decided to keep her baby when she had become pregnant out of wedlock. Ryan went on to college, played basketball and became Homecoming King at the college he attended. He now has a Masters degree and is married with two children. He also is a successful business man in pharmaceutical sales. "None of this would have happened if I hadn't chosen life," Glenna told me.

Because Glenna has a burden for the youth, she gladly works among them to help bring them to a saving knowledge of Jesus Christ. Once a year she coordinates a youth rally with the help of her church, where the students have an opportunity to hear the gospel and many have been saved. She also felt a calling from God to start a ladies Bible study in 1993 there in Groton that has been meeting for 20 plus years at her church.

Glenna concluded her testimony with me by sharing that the turning point in her life was when she became pregnant with Ryan. That was when she came back to the Lord and that was when she determined to remain with Him ever since. It was the love of God which was displayed towards her in that little charismatic church in Rapid City that made the big difference in Glenna's life. She gives God all the glory for what He has done in her life. Glenna says that **Matthew 6:33** has been her life verse, to always seek God first and He will take care of every need in your life.

Chapter 44

Pastor William (Bill) Duncan

1 John 4:12 – No one has seen God at any time. If we love one another, God abides in us, and His love has been perfected in us.

Bill was born in Dayton, OH. His father's parents, who emigrated from Ireland, were staunch Scotch-Irish Presbyterians. His mother's parents had gone to church occasionally when she was little but when the leaders of the church were found to be members of the Ku-Klux-Klan during the 1920's, Bill's maternal grandfather pulled his family out of the church and never entered any church again. He strongly disapproved of the way they were persecuting the Catholics in his neighborhood. Bill's paternal grandfather also felt that persecution of Catholics was wrong, and this was one of his reasons for immigrating to America from the religiously war-torn nation of Ireland in 1910.

Bill's father along with his four siblings turned their backs on their parents' faith and church as well by 1936. As a result when Bill's parents were married in 1937 neither of them returned to any worship services. They only set foot in the church when there was a marriage or a funeral. As a result, Bill's only experience with the church (except for being baptized as an infant in his grandparents' church) was when the next door neighbors asked his parents if they could take him to Sunday school. Bill was instantly enthralled by the excitement of being in 'school' at the age of three.

By the time Bill was 10 years old, the music director asked for his parents' permission to get Bill involved in the children's choir. Bill loved to sing from an early age. After he and his brother started singing in the choir, his parents started going back to church. They wanted to hear their sons perform. Eventually Bill's father recommitted his life to the Lord but as far as he knew his mother never did.

All through high school and college, Bill was very involved in the church. He loved everything about being in church; the music, the pomp, the acceptance by elders and peers, everything (he sees now) except the unconditional love and grace of God for His people. He joined the youth group, youth choir, helped out with the college ministry and even taught Sunday school. When he was 22 years old, he married his childhood friend and sweetheart, Jana.

Bill had graduated with a degree in Secondary Education but with the Viet Nam War going on and many seeking to avoid the draft by going into teaching, Bill found employment in that field very tight, but finally landed a job with the U.S. Army Materiel Command in Joliet, Illinois, and interned there before moving to his permanent assignment at the U.S. Army Tank Automotive Command in Warren, Michigan. Soon Bill and Jana became very involved with a wonderful suburban church there. All this time they were busy serving God without really knowing Him. They were God-fearing, God-worshipping, but not God-loving and trusting believers. This would soon lead into a crisis that lasted for two years.

Bill's father retired from his job in July of 1974 after forty-one years with GM. He had plans to spend more time with his two young grandchildren living in Michigan. He also was looking forward to doing volunteer work at the local hospital in Dayton. It was bright for the future in his life because he had hated his job, but was now free to really enjoy life. In fact, after signing his retirement papers on that Friday, he was heading home to pick up his wife and head for Michigan to see those two grandsons. But none of that was to be. As he was walking out of his work place for the last time, he collapsed on the sidewalk of a massive heart attack and died instantly. He was only 59-years-old.

When Bill received the news within the hour, he was devastated. His entire outlook on life was thrown into a tail spin and 'faith' in God was at that moment destroyed. He couldn't believe God would take his father just when he was about to embark on a life of enjoyment. This coupled with the fact that Bill hated his job exasperated the situation. He began to see himself working at his position for thirty years, hating it, and then on the day of his own retirement dying, having never really lived as he had wanted. Life no longer had meaning. Less than six months later when a close friend's young son collapsed and died suddenly of a heart condition, Bill's organs started shutting down. His kidneys quickly began showing signs of failing as his blood pressure shot through the roof, and his heart rate became extremely erratic. Bill began falling asleep at his desk from fatigue almost daily. He was suffering severe depression and committing, by his own mental submission, involuntary voluntary suicide as a result. Doctors told Jana that unless these physical problems were addressed, Bill would die within six months.

Jana was pregnant with their third child by this time and she was desperate. She fled to their pastor and close church friends and they counseled her in the Word of God and spent time in prayer with her. During a session with the pastor and his wife, she gave her heart totally to the Lord and was transformed inside. Bill noticed the difference in her life almost immediately. She no longer suffered from melancholia. Instead her countenance literally glowed with the joy and peace she felt inside. However this had no affect on him. He continued to suffer excruciating pain in his back from his malfunctioning kidneys which intensified his depression and continued to hang over him like a storm cloud. He attended church, sang in the choir, and fellowshipped with the church body, but inside, while happy for Jana, he was content to leave earth and leave behind the misery and oppression of his body and soul and just allow Jana to raise their children.

In May of 1976, Bill agreed to see the pastor who counseled him. "Whether you live or die you need to turn your life over to Jesus for your eternal soul," he warned. Then he opened up the Bible and read **John 14: 1-6** to him where Jesus spoke to His disciples saying, "Let not your heart be troubled; you believe in God, believe also in Me. In My Father's house are many mansions; if it were not so, I would have told you. I go to prepare a place for you. And if I go and prepare a place for you, I will come again and receive you to Myself; that where I am, there you may be also And where I go you know, and the way you know." The pastor continued reading and when he got to **John 14: 6** which said, "I am the way, the truth, and the life. No one comes to the Father except through Me," Bill broke down in tears. He let out all his pent up emotions, all his doubts, all his fears and laid them all at the feet of Jesus. Casting all his cares on Jesus he gave his life totally to Him and determined to put his entire trust in Him in Life or Death. It was as though a cement block had been lifted off his shoulders and the peace and joy of the Lord washed over and through him.

Four weeks later, Bill went back to the doctor who was amazed to find that he no longer had high blood pressure or a racing heart. When he took tests of his ailing kidneys they were found to be functioning completely normal. Bill had been healed not only spiritually, but physically. He was jumping, and leaping, and praising God!! The people at the church, amazed and rejoicing, noticed a welcome change in him. His birthday on May 18, 1976 was truly a celebration of his birth-day – his re-birth! What a joy enveloped this re-born 28-year-old husband!

A couple months later Bill and Jana were reminded of Robert Frost's poem "The Road Not Taken," as two consecutive messages from two family pastors began to tug at their heart. It was God speaking to them and calling them into the ministry. Bill attended seminary and became a pastor. In his first parish while in seminary, Bill and Jana realized how Bill's crisis a few years back had prepared them for His work. A fire at a supper club had taken thirteen lives in their community; five church members were among the lost. Understanding this sudden loss, as families and as church friends, though still a young man, Bill was able to be used by the LORD to minister God's healing love and restore the HOPE of Redemption to that devastated community, when all seemed lost and oh, so painful to endure.

Bill went on to pastor churches for 37 years and for 26 of those years he served the Groton/Houghton Christian & Missionary Alliance parish in South Dakota until he retired in June, 2014.

Bill and Jana have been blessed with seven children and twenty grandchildren to date. By the grace of God they have been able to enjoy these blessings to the fullest TOGETHER. Their youngest son was adopted when he was four years old. Three sons are pastors and their newly married son is preparing also to go to seminary in the fall of 2016. Six children and their spouses, all except for the youngest son, have chosen to serve the Lord. Grandchildren are also coming to know the wonderful saving grace of the LORD, and just recently, a granddaughter has asked Bill to accompany her on a mission trip to the Duncan ancestral country of Northern Ireland in June, 2016. Bill and Jana believe that because of all the love and prayers going up for their son and the grace being shown to him, he too will come to know the saving grace of Jesus as well. The LORD is faithful, and He will do it!

Chapter 45

Donna Seaton

Proverbs 3: 5-6 – Trust in the Lord with all your heart, and lean not on your own understanding; in all your ways acknowledge Him, and He shall direct your paths.

This is the way Donna has sought to follow Jesus all her life. She was born on December 17, 1926 in Aberdeen and lived near Sand Lake. Later the family moved to the little town of Stratford, just 15 miles south of Aberdeen. When Donna attended high school in Aberdeen she stayed at her grandmother's apartment house along with a roommate. The grandmother was a strong Christian and, therefore, a very positive influence on Donna. Early on Donna chose a life of sobriety, neither drinking nor smoking. Later on she married a man she had been dating for four years. He also was sober in his habits and followed her example in relying upon God for guidance. Together they brought four sons into the world.

The second boy was able to memorize scripture easily and this would prove to be very useful later on in life. At 17 years of age, he chose to follow the wrong path and started smoking and drinking. His life became a shambles as he spiraled downwards from then on. After he hit bottom many, many years later, he called his godly mother knowing that he would be received. "Mom, come get me," his quavering voice sounded over the phone. Donna immediately went to where he was. Soon she brought him home and he remained with her for seven years right up to his death three years ago. He loved cats and found a stray one wandering on the road. Immediately he brought it home. Donna wouldn't allow any cats or dogs in the house but she allowed her son to keep it in the garage.

This man struggled both physically and spiritually but Donna continued to pray for him. One night he came downstairs to where she was sitting and asked her to pray for him. He feared going to Hell as the Bible had stated no drunkard would enter the gates of Heaven so he forced himself to quit drinking. He had managed this for a week right up to the night he came to his mother for prayer. He had fallen and injured his shoulder so she rubbed it as she prayed for him. He quoted this scripture, "And whatever you ask in My name, that I will do, that the Father may be glorified." - **John 14:13** She had wanted to take him to a doctor when he had fallen but he refused to go. He just wanted prayer. He passed away that night and Donna believes that he had asked Jesus to take him home to be with Him. With an aching heart, Donna went out to the garage to feed his cat the following day and she heard a voice in her head saying, "Thank you, Mom!" This gave her the assurance that he went to Heaven to be with Jesus and that she will see him again someday.

Early in her life, two women came to her little church to start a small prayer group there. Donna took her youngest son and went to the meeting. She found it rather strange because she heard people praying in tongues for the first time. When they asked if she wanted to be filled with the Holy Spirit, she agreed. At first nothing appeared to happen because she didn't receive a prayer language. But some time later, on her way to the hospital to visit someone who was employed at the Senior Center where she worked, she was praying. Suddenly a foreign sounding word "Selah" came into Donna's mind and she spoke it out loud. As she repeated it other such words came and soon she found herself speaking in a strange language. This was to be the beginning of a new adventure in her walk with the Lord.

Donna helped to continue the prayer group in her church and it has been going on now for over 30 years. When the people gather together to pray, one of the ladies will write down the prayer requests and when they are answered she will record those as well. "There have been many answers to prayer," Donna told me. "One lady is in remission from cancer and we believe God has healed her."

Donna still remembers how the two ladies, who started the prayer group at church, would say to her every time she started to fret over something, "Donna, you are taking the care." These two dear friends have since gone on to be with the Lord but the prayer group has continued and it includes ladies from many denominations all over the city. This group is an extension of Aglow International and lately has become a Lighthouse Group. Aglow women and men reach into their local areas to feed the homeless, minister in jails and prisons, share Bible studies, work with orphans, reach out to juvenile facilities, nursing homes, hospitals and the list goes on as the possibilities for outreach are endless.

Chapter 46

Matt Gassen

Philippians 4:13 - I can do all things through Christ who strengthens me.

Like so many people in South Dakota, Matt was raised in a small farming community. His parents were hard working, giving people so Matt, at an early age, learned how to serve others. Although he was reared on Biblical principles he never learned the importance of being "born again." It would be much later in life before he would come to know Jesus as his true Lord and Savior.

After graduating from high school Matt worked three different jobs over the next couple of years. It was then that he and his wife, Charlene, began to struggle with what the future in their small town had to offer. Charlene had a desire to attend college but with no real skill set, Matt knew that would be challenging for their family. So Matt began to investigate other opportunities that would provide them with more choices. He finally made a decision to join the military and after talking to a few recruiters he settled on the Air Force. For the next 15 years he worked in the aircraft maintenance career field with assignments to Little Rock AFB, AR, Kadena AFB, Okinawa Japan and Mountain Home AFB, ID. He then took the opportunity to retrain to become a First Sergeant where he was responsible for the morale, welfare and conduct of all enlisted members in the squadrons he was assigned to. He derived a lot of pleasure out of this as he was able to counsel and help provide personal and career direction to hundreds of men and women that he supervised. First Sergeant Matt retired from the Air Force after nearly 23 years of service. He had served eight years as a First Sergeant.

It was during his time at Mountain Home AFB in Idaho where Matt's life made a dramatic change. Matt and Charlene were raised in a traditional denominational church. Charlene had been lead to the Lord by her brother several years prior and with her new found knowledge she struggled to continue attending the same church. So she began taking their sons and attending a church in the community of Mountain Home. In the beginning Matt stayed home, but then one Sunday he decided to go with Charlene. He was welcomed into the church and a wonderful couple there took him and Charlene under their wings and began mentoring them. This made a positive impression on Matt and he began to understand that there was a lot more to following Christ than mere ritual. After a year or so later, this couple left the church to attend a local full gospel church. Matt and Charlene followed them to the new church and this was where Matt made a personal decision to follow Jesus. After being baptized in the Snake River and filled with the Holy Spirit, Matt felt the warmth of new life wafting throughout his body. This was when he realized that God had a plan for his life and it had been there since before he was born.

The Holy Spirit was then able to take hold and lead Matt through several doors during the rest of his military career. After he retired from the Air Force he was blessed with the chance to become the Director of the Black Hills Regional Food Bank. Just 4 short years later God provided him the opportunity to become the Executive Director of the Food Bank in Sioux Falls, SD. Just over a year later a merger took place to combine the two existing food banks into one statewide hunger relief organization. Out of this merger, Feeding South Dakota was birthed. Matt believes his experience in the military and his home life as a child prepared him for this important work.

As a non-profit director he enjoys the blessings of being able to provide food to individuals and families who struggle to have enough to eat. One program that he runs provides back packs of food to needy children so they will have food over the weekends when they aren't in school and don't have access to school meals. Matt says that empty stomachs keeps children from reaching their greatest learning potential at school. Additionally, many senior citizens who subsist on social security alone are being helped through this organization as well. Although it isn't a faith based organization, Matt believes he is being used to reach people in practical ways so that their hearts will be softened to receive the gospel when God sends pastors and others to share the Word with them. As Matt was sharing, **I Corinthians 12** came alive to me as never before. I could envision how God was using each gift in the Body of Christ. It was like an orchestra with each person playing their own particular instrument to produce a great melody. This is how God wants people to use the gift He has given them and work together to accomplish God's purposes on this Earth and expand His Kingdom. It was easy to see how when one person fails in using his gift, the entire Body suffers. As I listened to Matt, it became clear to me that God had given him the gift of service. His job in the Air Force and his home life as a child prepared him for this as he watched his parents help others in so many practical ways.

Matt has learned to trust God for His provisions to carry on the work of Feeding South Dakota because often there is a lack of funds to meet all the needs. However God has always provided just at the right time through an unexpected donation or some other way.

Matt believes God has always guided him even before he knew Him personally. He has experienced His many blessings of having a wonderful wife who supports him and sons who have successful careers of their own. "I have always loved my work and that is a blessing in itself," Matt told me. "So many people hate their jobs." I knew that Matt loves what he does because he has been obedient in following the leading of the Holy Spirit.

I asked Matt if there were many who tried to use the system and he told me that he doesn't judge people's motives. He simply gives out food and knows when he gets to Heaven he will be greeted with "Well done, good and faithful servant!" He never wants to make a judgment and risk not helping someone who really needs it. I really learned something from this and was able to see how often I have judged others, not knowing their situation.

Matt ended his story this way. "We all start out with **John 3:16**. When I was first saved, I was able to understand the significance of that verse and how it has changed my life."

Chapter 47

Terrie Fischer

2 Corinthians 3:18 – But we all, with unveiled face, beholding as in a mirror the glory of the Lord, are being transformed into the same image from glory to glory, just as by the Spirit of the Lord.

Terrie was born in Dickinson, ND into a family of six children. She grew up in the church and learned all about God but didn't understand what it meant to receive Jesus into her heart as her Personal Savior. It wasn't until she was ten years old, when she and a sister were visiting an uncle that she was first introduced to Jesus. Before leaving on the bus for home, her uncle asked her if she wanted to invite Jesus into her heart and she did. However she wasn't discipled and she chose to follow her own way. At the young age of 14, she started drinking alcohol and smoking cigarettes. Soon she was experimenting with drugs. In turn this led to premarital sex, unwanted pregnancies and finally abortions. She, unknowingly, was seeking the love from men that could only be found in Jesus.

Terrie's life was filled with unhappiness and pain. By the time she was 27-years-old she was facing a second divorce. Her two children were from two different fathers – one from each marriage. She was carrying the heavy guilt of three abortions coupled with the emotional baggage brought on by the physical and mental abuse she had suffered in both marriages. Her addictions blinded her and she blamed others for her struggles in life.

Due to the drugs, domestic violence and spiritual bankruptcy, Terrie felt completely alone, confused, and totally lost. In May of 1981, she found herself in Keystone Treatment Center getting help for codependency. According to the Wikipedia Encyclopedia codependent relationships are a type of dysfunctional helping relationship where one person supports or enables another person's addiction, poor mental health, immaturity, irresponsibility, or under-achievement. Terrie had caused herself to place other peoples' opinions and values above her own and she was caught in the trap of sacrificing her own personhood for someone else's. Because she was so afraid of making someone angry, she would seek that person's approval above God's. She had weak personal boundaries and she was ashamed of not being able to stand up for herself. Things were about to change for Terrie.

The last night of her stay at Keystone, Terrie was still feeling lost and alone. She laid on her bed all curled up in the fetal position and she cried out to God, "I don't know who You are or what you are but I want You in my life." She repeated it again and again until her room suddenly filled with a white light. Out of the corner of her eye, Terrie saw Jesus standing to the left of her. A sense of peace filled her entire being and it was so strong she was overwhelmed. That intense sensation never came back but Terrie was determined that she would do whatever it took to know God. She then had a vision in which God showed her three things. First, she saw a twisted slinky along with several other slinkies in the same condition. She knew within herself that her life was like that slinky – all twisted up and unable to function the way she was created. Terrie also sensed God saying that she was trying to have relationships with people who were in the same twisted condition. The second thing she saw was a cross with a bright light emanating from it and two people who were lifting up a bundle. The third picture was two people circling around and around at the bottom of another cross of light. Terrie wondered about this vision and what it meant.

God showed her that He was the only one that could fix her slinky and help her have healthy relationships. He has been faithful to heal her heart and continues to provide her lasting fulfilling relationships. The first cross stood for Terrie's son's baptism. This was fulfilled eight weeks later. The second cross concerned her desire for a spiritual marriage. This occurred 1 ½ years later.

Since then, Terrie has been on a journey of being restored and being made into the image of Christ. She has had a heart for broken people ever since her conversion. Her desire to help others this way has been fulfilled as God has used her in this type of ministry. She has worked as a drug and alcohol counselor, working with broken families, parolees and teens. She has been on various missions' trips to Russia, Mexico and the Rosebud Indian Reservation. She has ministered to women who have undergone abortions and domestic violence, resulting in severe depression.

Currently, Terrie and her husband are leading a Celebrate Recovery Ministry in their church. It is part of a national interdenominational ministry that has been reaching millions of people through thousands of churches. People who are struggling come together to find help for their failing marriages and other various hurts, habits, and hang-ups. As the love of Jesus is displayed in the group, people begin to surrender and change. As they humble themselves and draw closer to God, they find healing and hope for their lives.

Terrie shared this last but not least important thing with me. "I give all glory to God for His faithfulness to draw back a 10-year-old girl to His heart. He has brought full restoration, peace and joy."

Chapter 48

Freida Fossum

John 15:15 – "No longer do I call you servants for a servant does not know what his master is doing; but I have called you friends, for all things that I heard from My Father I have made known to you."

Freida was born in Wichita, Kansas on September 24, 1947. Her mother and father divorced when she was only two years old so she went to live with her grandparents. Freida got used to wearing hand-me-downs because the family had little in material goods. Not only were they poor physically but spiritually as well. Freida remembers only one time when she went to church as a child and it turned out to be a very frightening experience. It was around Easter time and she heard that the church was giving away Easter lilies. She wanted one to give to her grandmother so she decided to go. The pastor was doing a series of sermons concerning the death, burial and resurrection of Jesus. Freida happened to get in on the one when Jesus was crucified on the cross. This was very scary to her because she left the church believing that Jesus was killed and left dead on the cross. She never went back to hear the rest of the story which was the good news that Jesus rose again to save her from her sins. She spent years and years of thinking that people were worshipping a dead person.

Freida married a man and had four children. His grandmother would bombard them with tracts and medals that she believed would keep them from going to Hell. But Freida didn't give it much heed. After divorcing this man a few years later, she met and married another man that she met at her workplace. They had one child together and this marriage lasted eight years before it broke up. During this time Freida thought nothing of telling dirty jokes, smoking, drinking and swearing. She would spend a lot of time with a friend who was a sworn atheist and they liked to poke fun at Christians. They would accuse them of worshipping a dead man and laugh at them. Freida believed that Christians were weak and running away from reality.

Things were about to change for Freida when she started taking her daughter to dance classes. It was during a dance seminar when she met Larry Fossum. He was so different from any of the other men she knew. He talked about Jesus and put Him before anything else in his life. Freida was taken aback and enthralled by all this so after Larry returned from a Promise Keepers meeting, her curiosity got the better of her. She asked Larry to take her to the church he was attending. It turned out to be a five-fold-ministry church where there was "laying on of hands" and dancing in the aisles with celebration of the Lord Jesus. As strange as everything seemed to Freida it didn't frighten her. In fact it was like meeting the family she had never known. After attending church there for two months, Freida learned that Jesus didn't just die on the cross and stay dead. Now she knew that He had risen from the grave and was Savior.

One night in May of 1994, Freida accepted Jesus as her Savior while she was alone in her trailer. For the next three hours she wrote down every word that God was impressing on her heart – words of direction for her life. She was so excited that she called Larry the very next morning as soon as she woke up. She was on the phone with him and read to him everything she had written down. From that day on Jesus replaced all the things in her life, including the rough language, with Joy and Love. Now He was and still is her best friend and she talks to Him all the time.

In 1997 when Freida was at a convention in Denver, she was filled with the Holy Spirit and received the gift of tongues. She was so transformed that her children accused her of being hypnotized.

Today Freida is married to Larry and she helps him pastor a church called the Cowboy Way Church. It has a Western culture and the services are held in a barn that has been transformed into a church. Freida is heavily involved in a women's ministry which has grown over the years. She and Larry have also embraced other ministries such as outreaches to rodeos, the reservations, and events of western culture such as rodeo Bible camp as well as a youth ranch that ministers to young girls. They are also joining a new young Native American pastor called Joe Marrowbone with his ministry. They love horses and have started an equestrian drill team that performs at rodeos to the accompaniment of Christian music. Between performances at the rodeos they have a table filled with Bibles, tracts, and other Christian material for people to take free of charge. Freida believes that many hearts are being touched at these events.

Although the membership at the Cowboy Way Church is small God has moved through healings and miracles. They have special meetings when an evangelist, Grant Gomez, comes to minister at least once a year. It was during these times when God moved powerfully in the services. A man and later on a woman were healed from terminal cancer. Also a boy with an enlarged heart was healed. Many lives have been changed as well as they received Jesus Christ into their hearts. Freida rejoices that she has chosen to move out of the dark and sinful life she had been living in and step into the light of Jesus her Savior and Lord.

Chapter 49

Rosemary Eliason

Isaiah 40:31 – But those who wait on the Lord shall renew their strength; They shall mount up with wings like eagles, They shall run and not be weary, They shall walk and not faint.

Rosemary was born in Salem, SD. She was destined by God to become a great prayer warrior and her prayers carried her and her family through many crises in her life. Here are some of the miracles that Rosemary shared with me.

It was winter and Rosemary's mother and father had gone to Salem to clean geese. They left Rosemary and her brother with farm neighbors. On the way home their parents ran into a blizzard and the visibility was very bad. Rosemary's father didn't see a truck that had stopped in the road and although he tried to swerve to miss it, he struck it on the side where Rosemary's mother was sitting. Rosemary didn't find out about her mother's tragic death until the next morning.

At the funeral, Rosemary's aunt lifted her up to see her mother in the coffin. She described how beautiful she looked in her snow white wedding gown. Rosemary remembers saying to the others, "Why are you crying. She is an angel now." In the future every time Rosemary would look at her mother's wedding picture, she would think, "Yes! That's just the way she looked – oh so beautiful." When she told her aunt about it, she told Rosemary, "No! Your mother wasn't buried in her wedding dress. She had on a rose-colored dress. You have her wedding dress in your cedar chest." Sixty years later, Rosemary met her mother's best friend who said to her, "Wasn't she beautiful all dressed in white. She was buried in her wedding dress you know." Rosemary told her she had seen her like that as well but she knew that was impossible because she had the wedding dress in her cedar chest. Rosemary believes this is how the Lord saw her in His eyes because white stands for purity.

Rosemary had a morbid fear of heights. Everywhere she went that was high up, she had to hold on to someone or something and close her eyes. She told me about the time she went to a conference held in a stadium which held 45,000 people. Because there were no seats available down below, Rosemary and the others who were with her had to go to the top of the stadium. Terrified, Rosemary grasped tightly to each one as she carefully shuffled her way to her seat. When she got there she was so petrified that she couldn't release her hands from the back of her seat. She so wanted to lift her hands in praise to the Lord but her hands would not let go. Suddenly Jesus appeared only two steps away from Rosemary with arms reaching out to her. He gathered her in His arms with His white robe covering her as she rested her head on His chest. A great sense of relief engulfed her as she stood there with Jesus. Then He vanished. Rosemary noticed that she was no longer afraid. She had been delivered from her phobia of heights. She rejoiced all the way back to her hotel. She tried to tell the others about her experience but they didn't believe her. Later on while traveling on the bus back home, a lady testified that she had seen Jesus walking among the aisles that night in the area where Rosemary had been sitting.

Rosemary's son, David, had a heart condition that caused an irregular heartbeat. Rosemary's husband had passed away from the same condition. When David had an attack, he was rushed to the hospital where he was stabilized. They gave him some medicine but warned him that it could cause bleeding. He took it any way the same night he had been discharged from the hospital. The blood vessels burst and he began to bleed from his mouth and nose. It took four days back at the hospital for the doctors to stop the bleeding. They did emergency surgery where they went through David's groin into his head to cauterize the blood vessels. In the mean time Rosemary prayed in earnest and called on her prayer warrior friends to pray as well. Rosemary believes that God used the doctors to save her son's life.

The next night Rosemary was brought out of her sleep to a sitting position in bed where she saw her deceased husband. "I'm just stopping in to check up on you," he said. Rosemary described him as looking like a 30-year-old man. "He wasn't old or overweight. Instead he was filled with joy and delight and he looked radiant. I have never seen him look like that on this side of Heaven."

After Dennis had passed away, the Lord said to Rosemary, "You are now the matriarch of the family. Go and pray a blessing over each member of your family." Rosemary did and as she finished praying for her daughter, her daughter saw a "circle of light." A dog, that had died, appeared in the center of the circle and the shadow of a person walked towards it. As soon as he had stepped into it, the circle closed up into a ball of light and floated off into the distance. This occurred at the same time a nurse had come into the hospital room to check on Dennis. "He is gone," she remarked.

Rosemary and Dennis, her husband, along with a couple of their grandchildren were driving home from the Turner County Fair. Dennis was driving around 80 miles an hour. It was night time so a black cow standing in the middle of the road was very difficult to see. Rosemary knew that if they kept going straight they would hit the cow and if they swerved to miss it, the car would roll. Either way would spell sudden disaster for the family. "Help us, Jesus," Rosemary cried over and over again. Jesus answered that prayer because the car miraculously missed the cow and the occupants of the car were spared.

Rosemary prayed for everyone and everything, even her pets. They had a poodle which got very ill. When they took her to the veterinarian he took a picture of her stomach and discovered a ball of string. The vet told Rosemary and Dennis that the dog would need surgery and it would cost $200. Rosemary and the children were in tears. The veterinarian took the poodle to the hospital and used some of their equipment to take another picture. As the vet was taking the dog to the hospital, Rosemary told her family to pray as they never prayed before. Soon he informed Rosemary and Dennis that all he could see was a red spot and the dog would be fine. It amazed the vet because he knew he had seen the ball and the dog hadn't vomited it up nor passed it otherwise. God had healed the poodle. Rosemary saw another of her dogs healed through prayer as well. The dog had injured its leg and couldn't walk on it. As soon as Rosemary prayed for it, it started running around on all fours. God had healed it.

Rosemary was very happy at the church she was going to and she wasn't about to change. God had other ideas, however, and He spoke to her about going to another church. Rosemary refused to go because the church had no life in it. When she had disobeyed God it was as if a cold blanket came down out of Heaven and rested on her. She noticed that there was a rift between God and herself. This frightened her so she told God, "Ok Lord! If you want me to go to that church just tell me again and I will do it." Later Rosemary was invited by a friend to attend a conference at another church in town. After the speaker spoke, the Lord told Rosemary to walk up to the preacher because he had her answer. As she walked up there were at least 75 people who divided like the Red Sea and she just talked through the 6 – 10 foot opening. As she approached the speaker, he pointed his finger at her and said, "You there are to go to ____ ____. When he said that, Rosemary became aware of a black cloud breaking open over her head. She could see angels dancing with joy in the opening of the cloud. As she was driving home she felt like she was driving Santa's sleigh. As she rounded the corner of the church she was to attend, she heard the Lord say to her, "Some people are sent to the mission field. This church is your mission field.

The next day, Dennis told Rosemary he wanted the children to be confirmed. Rosemary agreed and told him they could try "this church," knowing it was the one God had told her to attend. She turned her back to Dennis so he couldn't see her smile. Rosemary discovered that the pastor was spirit-filled and the services were anointed. This pastor asked her to be on the prayer team and Rosemary gladly accepted. She knew now why God had wanted her to go to that church. He had called her to be a prayer warrior. This was her gift and God wanted her to use it.

Chapter 50

Edith Gwien

Romans 10:15 – How beautiful are the feet of those who preach the gospel of peace, Who bring glad tidings of good things!

Edith was born in Liberia, Africa along with four brothers and four sisters. Four of her siblings are still living today. She also has nine children and twenty-three grandchildren. Her mother and father were married for 67 years before they went on to be with the Lord.

Edith has experienced several miracles during her life. She told me about the time in 1982 when she was pregnant and became ill. When she first went to the doctor he told her the baby was fine. But later on Edith found out the baby wasn't ok. In fact it was turned the wrong way in her womb. Edith was in great pain for two days and then on February 9th she went to the hospital. When the doctor came and checked her he told her that she needed a cesarean. Edith went into a room to put on a hospital gown to get ready for surgery. Suddenly the door closed and locked behind her. The doctor and nurses weren't able to enter the room. Edith looked around and suddenly four angels in dazzling white robes appeared before her. Their hair was white and they were covered in a brilliant light. One of the angels touched her on her stomach where the baby was. As soon as he touched her the baby was born and the angel tied the umbilical cord with a brilliant white string. As soon as he tied the other end of the cord, he cut it. Then the angels disappeared and the door opened. Doctors and nurses came running. When they found out what happened, they were amazed at the miracle. As a result 40 of them were saved, including the head nurse. This news reached the TV, radio and newspaper. People began to visit Edith and asked her to pray for them.

A month later, Edith became paralyzed and was unable to walk. The doctor told her she would never walk again. Edith prayed and told God, "You delivered me before. You can do it again." God heard her and three months later, Edith was walking. Edith praised God and danced before Him and she does this at church to this day.

God called Edith to pray for people and she has seen many people healed. One time, she met a lady and her husband who had been married for nine years but were childless. God told her to go and pray for them. He also told her to take a green cup with her because He wanted the couple to drink water from a green cup. When Edith arrived at the couples' house, she thought they would drink the water from the cup she had brought but the lady brought out another green cup from her kitchen. God had done this so the lady would know that He had sent Edith to pray for her. As a result she had the faith to believe. Three months later, Edith got word that the lady had conceived. Her husband came to see Edith and he told her that he would do anything for her because he was so grateful. Edith told him that she only wanted him to give all thanks and glory to the Lord.

One day Edith had a vision of Jesus and a long line of people standing there from all over the world. There was a big book the size of a city sitting there along with a pen. Jesus told the people who believed in Him to stand at His right hand side and for the unbelievers to stand at His left. The believers were shining bright and the others on Jesus' left side were dark. Jesus revealed to Edith that He is coming soon and He wants her to share His gospel with everyone before it is too late.

God has put His mantel of protection upon Edith so she can carry out His mission. When she and her family were still in Liberia and war broke out in 1990, the enemy entered their home. The soldiers meant to do them harm but God warned them not to hurt them. After that the commander told his soldiers to leave that house alone. Ever since then, Edith has known God's hand of protection upon her. Every time the enemy tries to harm her whether it is in a car accident or some other way, God has always come to her rescue.

People are always calling Edith to come and pray for them. She prays for people in Africa as well as here. God has put it on Edith's heart to pray especially for California, Texas, and South Dakota. God has warned her that unless the nation repents of its many sins destruction will come.

Chapter 51

Gary Allen

1 Corinthians 4:1 – Let a man so consider us, as servants of Christ and stewards of the mysteries of God.

Gary was born in St Louis, MO to godly parents. His father served as a deacon and treasurer in his church. Gary grew up in the church and he was always aware of the presence of God. At age seven he made a decision to follow Jesus and invited Him into his heart. At age eleven he was filled with the Holy Spirit and soon after sensed the calling of God to become a pastor.

Gary married a Christian lady by the name of Arlene. Together they followed the Lord's leading to pastor their first church in Central Illinois. During this time in their first church, Arlene became pregnant. Around the fifth month, she began bleeding. The doctor did everything he could to try to stop the hemorrhaging and he put Arlene on complete bed rest. She managed to carry the baby to full term and gave birth to their first son. During the process of giving birth, she nearly died from a loss of blood despite the transfusions.

During their ministry in their second church, Gary and Arlene lost two babies each at around the 5th month of pregnancy. She still struggled with the bleeding and the doctor strongly urged Arlene to have a hysterectomy. Arlene and Gary refused because they wanted more children. Instead they decided to trust God. A year later Arlene became pregnant again and around the 5th month, the bleeding started again. Arlene and Gary went to church that night and asked for prayer. An older gentleman prayed for Arlene and then gave her a word from God. He told her the bleeding would stop and she would carry the baby to full term. It would be a boy and she was to name him John. Gary told Arlene that if this was truly a word from God that it would come to pass. Everything happened as the older man at church had said. When Arlene went into labor she went to the hospital fully expecting a girl to be born. Instead she had a boy and she and Gary named him Richard Jon (rather than the traditional John).

Despite the fact that Gary led a godly life, he had his share of problems. When he was only 16 years old his mother passed away. Later on his father was stricken with dementia and went to live with Gary and Arlene for five years until his death.

Gary R. Allen, DMin., has served as pastor, US Navy Chaplain, police chaplain, National Director for Ministerial Enrichment for the Assemblies of God and currently serves as chaplain for the employees of the National Office of the Assemblies of God.

Chapter 52

My Brush With Death

Psalm 118:17 – I shall not die, but live, And declare the works of the Lord.

Little did I know when I went along with my husband and a medical team to help the people in Peru, that I would be dangerously close to never seeing home again.

I was excited to be able to see the Peruvians again after so many long years had passed since we had been there once before. I always loved the Spanish speaking people and I tried to learn as much of their language as I could so I could communicate with them even if it was on a very simple level.

When we arrived in Peru, we were introduced to the missionaries there right away. The doctors there who would join our medical team were very friendly and made us feel right at home.

My husband helped out in the pharmacy by dispensing simple over-the-counter drugs such as aspirin while I worked with the prayer team. I was amazed at how spiritually hungry the people there were. Every person that I asked if they wanted me to pray with them to receive Christ eagerly accepted. After prayer a card was filled out so somebody could follow up on that person and get him or her involved in the church. In Peru, when a person accepts Jesus as their Savior he is immediately assigned to a small group where he can be discipled.

During the excitement of this adventure, I didn't heed the doctor's advice to drink plenty of fluids. I was too busy praying for people to give it much thought. I figured that the coffee I drank in the mornings would suffice.

After days of enjoying the Peruvian cuisine of alpaca, ostrich and other foods that were strange to us, I somehow picked up a viral intestinal illness. It was a day or two before our departure back to the States when

I felt weak and needed to lie down. When my doctor listened to my heart, he told me my heartbeat was abnormally high and gave me a pill to help slow it down. He wanted me to get my heart checked out after returning home.

The last day, we boarded a tour bus to enjoy the sites of the city before going to the airport for our departure home. Little did I know before climbing the stairs to the upper deck of the bus that I was about to embark on one of the most frightening experiences of my life. We were sitting there and receiving hats to help keep the hot Peruvian sun off our faces. The elevation was quite high as well. Suddenly and without warning, I began to feel very weak and faint. I had to lay down. The next thing I knew I was struggling for oxygen. It felt like someone had put a pillow case over my head. I gasped and sucked in air but it didn't seem to do any good. I felt like I was suffocating. My doctor took my blood pressure and it was sinking. Every few minutes he took it again to discover that it was steadily dropping until it was reaching dangerous levels. Eventually it sank so low he couldn't even get a reading. I was in deep, deep trouble.

In the mean time, my doctor's wife, Stephanie, pleaded with the bus driver to hurry up and get to the nearest hospital. Luckily there was one only three blocks away. However the bus driver would not budge. "Everyone has to be strapped in or I can't move this bus," he replied. In desperation, Stephanie told him that is was a matter of life and death. Then he started the bus. When she returned by my side everyone was feeling frantic inside even though they presented a calm demeanor. Not knowing what else to do, they all began praying for me. As soon as they finished praying my blood pressure began to rise. When the bus arrived at the hospital I was finally able to sit up. With help I managed to reach the bottom of the stairs of the bus where I passed out cold. The next thing I knew I was on a gurney being wheeled into the emergency room.

After receiving IV fluids for my dehydration, my doctor hoped I would be strong enough to fly back home but I felt very sick and weak. My husband and I had to remain back in Peru while the rest flew back to the States. We stayed in our hotel room and the Peruvian doctor ordered a private nurse for me. Every couple of hours, she would awaken me and make me drink fluids with electrolytes in them. After a couple of days I was able to make the trip home.

Every year thousands of people are hospitalized due to dehydration. Hundreds more die. I was foolish enough not to take my doctor's advice seriously and I was nearly one of those statistics. I thank God He gave me another chance. Unbeknownst to me, during my crisis in Peru, Stephanie had prayed **Psalm 118:17**, inserting my name into it. Little did she realize that she was praying a prophetic prayer over me. God wanted me to declare His works by penning the testimonies of those in my first book, "Living Stones" and later on in this one.

As of this writing I am 80 years old and plan to keep on following and obeying Him right up to my last breath.

Conclusion

Perhaps as you read these stories, you were able to relate to some of the people who shared. This book was written to encourage you and bring you hope. You may be in what seems to be a hopeless situation but I want you to know that God is a God of the impossible. If you just hang in there and keep praying and not give up, the Lord will walk with you all the way through to the other side. I know how you must feel discouraged and afraid when you find yourself in the middle of a storm. I have been there many times and have seen God move in ways I never dreamed of. If you are a Christian, you have the hope of Jesus, a hope those without Him do not have. I hope you will take this book and share it with people you have been praying for, people who need a boost right now as well as those who haven't committed themselves to Christ.

If you don't know Jesus Christ as your personal Savior and Lord, I have good news for you. You don't have to wait until you are good enough. You never will be good enough and that is why Jesus came and died on a cruel cross for you. It makes no difference what you have done or how badly you have sinned. Jesus has His arms stretched out to you beckoning you to come to Him. You can come just as you are. Don't worry about cleaning yourself up. He will do that. All you need to do is say this simple prayer.

"Dear Jesus,

I know I have sinned against You and I am sorry. I need you, Lord, because I know I can never earn my way to Heaven. Please come into my heart and take over my life. I am tired of going my way. Now I want to go Your way. I want to live for You and I want my life to bring glory to You. Please forgive me and wash me clean. Thank you, Jesus, for dying for me. Amen!"

If you have prayed that prayer, God wants you to tell somebody. Jesus said in **Matthew 10:32**, "Therefore everyone who confesses Me before men, I will also confess him before My Father who is in heaven." The next thing you should do after praying that prayer is to get baptized in water. If you were baptized as an infant, you still need to get baptized as a believer. Baptism doesn't save anybody but it is a way of confessing to others that you are a believer and have put your trust in Jesus Christ for your salvation. It will seal in your heart what you have just done. Jesus commanded His disciples in **Matthew 28:19** to baptize believers in the name of the Father, Son, and Holy Spirit. Baptism also demonstrates how the believer's old life has been buried with Christ when he goes down under the water.   When he comes back up, it symbolizes how, through faith, the believer has been raised with Christ. (See **Colossians 2:12**) It is also very important to find a good Christ centered church that teaches the Word of God. May God bless you in your new walk with Him!